Praise for *Connected Leadership*

"Francis Eberle's unique model of collaboration for *Connected Leadership* provides a framework for thinking and taking action that will benefit every leader."

—Marshall Goldsmith, Thinkers50 #1 Executive Coach and the only two-time #1 Leadership Thinker in the world

"Leadership skills must evolve to engage our cross-generational workforce teams to achieve business goals. The *Connected Leadership* model will guide leaders through the leadership evolution."

—Connie Yuen, Vice President of Finance, GreatHorn, Inc.

"2020 has shown the extreme need for nontraditional, flexible, and collaborative leadership to overcome unpredictable events. Dr. Eberle's *Connected Leadership* teaches how to engage self-leading teams."

—Ramin Karimpour, Founder and CEO of Applied LifeSciences & Systems

"In *Connected Leadership*, Francis Eberle goes beyond simply highlighting the value of collaborative, servant leadership—he offers practical guidance on how leaders can effectively connect with their teams and stakeholders."

—Brian MacLeod, Wayfair Head of Specialized Service

"Strong relationships help you tap into a diverse matrix of thoughts, making you a more competent and confident leader who can effectively lead others to their purpose. A clear purpose will engage the power of the team."

—Gretchen McDade, Vice President/General Manager, Sales, Constellation Brands

"Each decision a leader makes has a ripple effect. *Connected Leadership* clarifies the benefits to an organization of a collaborative leader who works in a connected fashion. This skill is essential for all leaders."

—Mark R. Proctor, M.D., Neurosurgeon-in-Chief, Boston Children's Hospital, Franc D. Ingraham Professor of Neurosurgery, Harvard Medical School

"Francis Eberle gets at the heart of collaborative leadership with authenticity and simplicity. It is a must read to succeed in our planned collaborative efforts with others."

—Sadhana Hall, Deputy Director, Nelson A. Rockefeller Center for Public Policy and the Social Sciences

"I loved the ideas Francis Eberle shared with us about collaborative leadership in today's new workplace. He is a smart and seasoned leader and that comes through in *Connected Leadership*."

—Ron Price, Founder, President & CEO, Price Associates

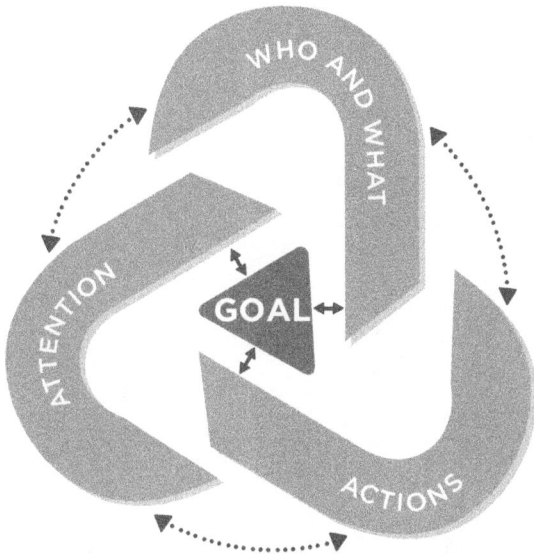

Ecosystem

WHO AND WHAT

ATTENTION

GOAL

ACTIONS

Workforce

CONNECTED LEADERSHIP

ENGAGE YOUR WORKFORCE TO LEAD THEMSELVES

Francis Eberle, Ph.D.

Connected Leadership
Engage Your Workforce to Lead Themselves
By Francis Eberle, Ph.D. © 2021

Hardcover ISBN: 978-1-61206-223-5
Softcover ISBN: 978-1-61206-224-2
eBook ISBN: 978-1-61206-225-9
Digital Download Edition ISBN: 978-1-61206-226-6

Cover and Interior Design by: Fusion Creative Works, FusionCW.com
Lead Editor: Megan Terry

To purchase this book at quantity discounts, contact Aloha Publishing at
alohapublishing@gmail.com

Published by

ALOHA
PUBLISHING

Printed in the United States of America

To my wife, Diane, for our many years of collaboration.

Contents

As a leader, you must make daily choices about how to use your authority. If you understand that leadership is a privilege and others know more than you in their areas of expertise, you can shift your focus from what you can achieve to how you can enable others on your team to achieve organizational goals.

Dyslexia made me think differently about tasks and processes, and learn to experiment with alternatives and look for assistance to get things done. Being different didn't stop me from achieving leadership roles, and I have learned that thinking differently is a positive trait in business.

The wide-ranging skills and knowledge needed to advance in our technologically driven society make collaboration across disciplines mandatory. It promotes innovation for solving complex, multidimensional problems. My model for collaboration demonstrates how this works.

The goal is the most important part of the collaboration model. When the goal is clear, partners, suppliers, contractors, and providers know who you are and whether you are a competitor. In circumstances where the future is unclear, you can develop the goal based on what you know.

Collaboration requires more than skills and knowledge. Building a collaborative environment is about choosing people who have skills in working with others. You must look at how they can grow rather than limiting your view to their past experiences and skills.

Finding a path to the goal requires determining the actions needed and the milestones required to measure progress. You must understand how the collaboration will work and adapt the plan as the work develops.

In the digital world, you must adapt the way you work with technology rather than maintaining the old work patterns. You must apply attention during a collaboration to monitoring, observing, adapting, searching for people's talents, and acknowledging and celebrating milestones.

A collaborative effort is going well if the problems and challenges are mostly handled at the level where they arise. Conflicts can result in better products or stronger partnerships, if people are willing to stay focused on the goal.

Being an infinite learner is a mindset that keeps you looking for new information and solutions—it keeps you flexible and curious. This attitude is critical to being a connected leader.

Self-awareness of emotions and mindset can help you avoid allowing others to derail you. Observe the team's progress so you can act before they get off track.

You need a high level of trust among all participants to create a true collaboration. Trust and honesty are values, not directives. Competition among team members destroys trust when individuals work to "win" at the expense of others.

Introduction

*"Never doubt that a small group of thoughtful,
committed citizens can change the world; indeed,
it is the only thing that ever has."*

—Margaret Mead

Most organizations value collaboration and teamwork, and yet many of them fail to implement these techniques and approaches when and where it matters most—in their leadership style. I wrote this book because I have observed that our leaders and organizations have knowledge and intelligence they are not using. Knowing how to tap into this intelligence is a modern leadership skill. The key to unlocking that intelligence is *connected leadership*, a type of collaboration.

A successful business or project of any kind does not rely solely on one person. It requires others and often an entire ecosystem to operate properly, which includes any number of people and environments in which the project takes place. All of these people and related factors must be accounted for and treated properly to create successful connected leadership.

Some think of collaboration as putting people together and giving them a task to work on along with leadership roles. However there's a distinction between a group of people in a workplace and a team. Simply working together is not collaboration. A group of people is just a group until they share principles and goals—then they are a team that is capable of teamwork.

This book is based on my experiences in leadership roles, research in the field of leadership, and the experiences of colleagues and partners.

You may have heard the term "collaborative leadership" before. It's not a new concept. My hope is to give you a new model for understanding how well connected leadership works in the current complex business ecosystem—a business environment that has been transformed by advanced digital technology.

I will occasionally use both connected and collaborative leadership synonymously. Connected leadership is a type of collaborative leadership with an emphasis on providing opportunities for others to lead. Connected leadership focuses on sharing authority.

My experience and learning in leadership began in high school, where my peers elected me to a leadership position. This was a boarding school which I was privileged to attend. One of the benefits to me was their governance structure, as the senior students essentially ran the operations of the school. The seniors were given authority over the younger students, who did much of the daily maintenance and upkeep. Imagine today giving students the authority of faculty and administrators. It was a unique way to share leadership.

My role was oversight of the living facilities. There were around 150 students total, with no custodians, no dishwashers, and no groundskeepers. If there was work to do that didn't require heavy machinery or technical expertise, students were expected to step in and do the work. For behavior infractions, a student discipline council would make decisions about punishments. Minor offenses were brought to a student board of discipline and they would determine the consequences. Faculty stepped in on this process only if an abuse of the system was egregious. This model worked as long as the seniors accepted and honored their leadership in an ethical and honest fashion without abusing their power. At this young age, I observed how people acted when given authority.

I mention this period in my life because I experienced firsthand at an impressionable age the good and bad of leadership. This helped me realize leadership is a privilege and leaders have a responsibility to not overuse their authority.

> **Collaborative leadership is knowing when to step up and when to step back.**

Leaders have daily choices about what to do with their authority. In that school, I saw seniors make younger students do extra chores, do pushups, and even play cruel games. My role was to act if I saw something. At that age, I decided I would use my authority to support others, build capacity, encourage resolution, solve problems, ignore small policy infractions that only would get broken again, and act decisively if the infraction was dangerous or hateful. Those choices and values have stayed with me ever since that time.

In my first career as a teacher, I soon began to lead other teachers in learning new techniques and strategies. Looking for other opportunities, I left teaching to lead a startup science museum, which led to taking over the leadership of a nonprofit organization that was teetering on the edge of ruin after losing two-thirds of its budget. We started over and in 10 years we were serving clients nationally and had established ourselves as a national voice in science and mathematics educational practices.

From there, my role was to lead the National Science Teaching Association in Washington, D.C., with 300,000 members, almost 1,000 volunteers, and 100-150 staff. Before leaving D.C., I worked as an assistant executive director for state policy with state boards of education and federal and state government. I have been on many boards of directors for national organizations and smaller regional ones. It was always a pleasure to be in the service of others to help them accomplish their missions, over these many years.

I saw many leaders treat their roles as an almost-sacred agreement with the people they served. I also observed adults behaving very much like some of the high school students, abusing authority, controlling, protecting power, discrediting and demeaning others, and acting unethically. This was true in both the private and public sectors. My fundamental leadership principles of sharing the role and working with others were my approach to building a foundation for longer-term opportunities. Others can help you accomplish much more than you can accomplish alone.

If team members share the same principles and a focused goal, they can be effective as a team. Otherwise they are only a group.

Every decision by a leader, however small, has implications for other people. Remembering that my actions were observed, judged, and reacted to made me realize the humility necessary for leadership roles, along with a willingness to accept the consequences of those decisions. You can't get anything done without others. Building partnerships and relationships helps clients, businesses, government, and customers to become more engaged and positive.

Building this model of leadership is a long-term process. Listen and involve others to make decisions. Be patient and look for ways to help others grow and learn. Leverage the expertise of others to the benefit of all parties.

I have entered every leadership position I've taken as if it were temporary. Whether a board member or an executive, every leader moves on, and reminding yourself of that helps you focus on the future of the organization rather than your own future.

Now I am an executive coach and team dynamics specialist. I help leaders reflect on their own experiences and knowledge and effectively connect to people and organizations to develop solutions. I like to say I help others see and understand things they may not have recognized to help them grow.

How Is Connected Leadership Different?

This is a book for leaders about the *application* of leadership. Consider your path in leadership. Did you get those opportunities by yourself? How do you work with others? What do you ultimately want: your success or the success of the organization? A good leader's success is the success of those they lead. It's often difficult to let others take the credit because expectations for a leader are usually based on traditional, authoritative models of leadership.

Leaders are confronted with many complex problems. Getting complex tasks done is hard. Our brains are only so big. We can conceive of big things such as a merger, new product lines, expansions, or an innovation, but to make these goals happen requires the help of others.

Others are more motivated to help if they feel you are behind them, give them some authority, and support them. You really don't have to do all the work, but simply clear the way for the work to be done.

The traditional directive leadership approach is simple: telling others what to do. The drawbacks to this are well documented: employees don't know why the task is needed; they don't have ownership; and often all the risk and consequences are on them, leading to an unmotivated or even destructive workplace. This sink-or-swim method confuses employees about the direction, purpose, and benefits of the job.

Like directive leadership, collaborative leadership sometimes requires being decisive, acting quickly, or setting direction. The difference between these styles is the mindset about the tasks the leader takes on.

Collaborative leadership is thinking about your leadership role and when to step up or step back.

There are paradoxes in leadership. You need to be humble, innovative, strategic, traditional, technology savvy, systems-minded, and political. These ideas are adapted from global services company PwC's 2018 article by Blair Sheppard called the "Six Paradoxes of Leadership," addressing the crisis of leadership. These are qualities of a strong collaborative leader:

Humble: Step back and allow others to support, direct, and take credit. Listen and act.

Innovative: Think toward the future while knowing an innovation can be a slight change in a current process or product rather than a large-scale change.

Strategic: Keep goals in mind at all times and implement processes effectively without forgetting where you want to go.

Traditional: It will always be necessary to remain decisive and competitive. There are times when these traditional values are needed.

Technology savvy: Know enough to communicate and be aware when new methods are effective or distracting from the goal.

Systems-minded: The world is complex. Understand that strategies, tactics, and partner interactions will impact people, functions, and/or results.

Political: Move among and around decisions or relationships with flexibility so you continuously move toward your goal.

Because of the various roles a leader plays, having others to help lead is critical today. Solving complex problems using other people's thinking, capacity, analysis, and implementation allows actions and authority to be distributed. Employees play an important role in idea generation, task implementation, and monitoring. This results in quicker decision-making, rather than sending decisions "up the ladder."

In a traditional organizational structure with decisions being sent up or down the chain of command, a decision can be delayed before the executive hears of it. There is greater shared responsibility with a collaborative style as the participants are accountable to each other and the leader. Employees know they will let each other down if they do not complete their tasks. If a leader makes the decision alone, others can second-guess the choice, place blame, or say it is not their job.

Many people are cautious of collaboration because accountability is distributed across multiple people. They worry that if there is no chain of command with accountability at the top, then no one is accountable. However, accountability can be designed into the project and adjusted throughout the process so there is greater accountability among the participants. It also keeps accountability closer to the decisions and actions rather than waiting until the end of a project or task. When there is a delay or error, solutions can be explored at the level of the action, and the responses can be imple-mented more quickly. If the consequences of not doing something correctly apply to the project or goal rather than the individual, employees will work harder to succeed.

Companies have long struggled to break down silos and boost cross-functional collaboration, but the challenge is getting more acute. Much about the world is unknown and changing, and we have to act regardless of what we know or don't. The speed with which companies need to respond to the changes of our modern business ecosystem requires rapid adaption of their products, servic-es, and experiments. Customers increasingly want an organization to present them with a coherent face. If businesses don't adapt, their interaction with customers becomes sluggish, customized products are hard to create on time and on budget, and blocked lines of communication make new sales and distribution channels difficult to navigate.

Set Direction With the End in Mind

In 2011, I sat in a coffee shop, looking across the street at the old White House office building with a staff person from the White House Office of Science and Technology Policy (OSTP), discussing a project to catalyze people around the country. I was part of a team helping develop a distribution project similar to a GoFundMe site, which didn't exist at that time. The OSTP had no money to put toward the project—just their vision. The vision of this project was powerful and challenging.

The project could potentially greatly change the amount of funding for teachers to do projects with their students. On aver-age, at the time, teachers spent $479 of their own money on school supplies, and they spent more on special projects. The OSTP first wanted input about the design of the project and opinions on the viability of it. Second, they were looking for partners. These were weighty concerns and would take time to consider.

When dealing with a White House-launched project, everyone involved has to be vetted multiple times. My credibility and the reputation of the organization I represented were on the line as well as that of the OSTP staff person if anything went wrong. The risks were high, but the potential benefit was also high, both for the teachers who would receive the support and for the partners who did the good work. The speed at which White House staff moves is faster than anyone I have ever met. They wanted to act as quickly as they could and with little room for error.

We agreed to partner and the project was launched. Within a few months, many teachers and their students around the country benefited from the support they were given. We could not commit money—only time. This project tested my collaborative leadership skills in obtaining the commitment and buy-in of the outside players, both businesses and foundations, to jump in and take on tasks. In some cases, it involved their own money—there was no return for them in terms of direct revenue. What made this project work with no funding? The model for collaboration that we used is the subject of this book.

I stayed in touch with the staff person after he left the OSTP, and not long after, he sent me a photo of a whiteboard. On it was the operating principles for their team at OSTP, which greatly helped their internal process. Here are some examples from the list:

▶ Think of the end at the beginning.

▶ Steer. Don't row.

▶ An entrepreneur is someone not limited by the resources directly under their control.

▶ Strong relationships are built on trust, mutual understanding, and reciprocity.

▶ Don't be a bottleneck.

▶ You can get more things done if you do not care who gets the credit.

These operating principles are all about setting direction with the end in mind and not interfering in the process. They clarify some of the ideas needed to work with others collaboratively.

As a leader, would you be able to operate by the OSTP's principles listed above? This book will put these principles in a framework that is more concrete and illustrate which are leadership skills and which are mindsets.

The OSTP team I worked with handled thousands of emails, calls, and requests and attended an incredible number of meetings each day. How did this project succeed when their priorities were so vast? They had no money. The challenges they faced were really not within their control. They could only control the vision and leverage others by sharing what was possible. The vision and its potential were a powerful draw.

1

Seeing Differently

"You see, but you do not observe. The distinction is clear."

—Sherlock Holmes, from *A Scandal in Bohemia*
by Sir Arthur Conan Doyle

When I was 11 years old, my parents were worried about my school performance because I was having trouble writing and reading. I was not a troublemaker—if anything, I was too quiet and introverted and often forgotten by teachers. Even though I read constantly, I was still a slow reader. I was also a bad speller, but I didn't realize it until about age 15. Poor spelling still plagues me today. At age 11, my confidence had not yet been diminished by others telling me I was not good at reading or spelling or English.

My parents took me to a child psychologist who gave me a battery of learning and aptitude tests. I remember enjoying one of them in particular, which asked what I saw in an ink spot. I always saw something. The result of long assessments described me as very intelligent, and gave me a high IQ score, but based on the norms of the tests, I had a learning disability: dyslexia.

My parents worked hard to find additional learning opportunities for me. I didn't notice any improvement in school as the tutors used the same rote learning and practice techniques I experienced in school. That is not my learning style. In those days, dyslexia was not well understood and special education was only for severely learning-disabled students. I had to learn to accept the criticism that I was not a good writer, reader, or speller without really understanding why.

I truly began to understand my dyslexia in high school. It took me much longer to read assignments than other students, and spelling was a problem for me. Some psychologists say there is a "square root rule" for people with dyslexia, meaning it takes a dyslexic person the square root longer to learn something. In other words, if a non-dyslexic person took two hours to learn something, it would take four hours for a dyslexic person to learn it. I had to adjust my time commitments (and I still do) to reflect how long I thought it would take me to complete assignments. I also realized I needed to write and rewrite, rewrite, and rewrite again before submitting any written assignment.

School has always been a challenge for me. Even though it was difficult, I spent many years in school. You might think I was crazy, but I pursued a terminal degree. While pursuing my doctorate, I handed in my first paper to a professor I highly respected. After he read it, he asked me if English was my second language. That was a shocker. However, after 20 years of school, I was quite immune to outwardly reacting to negative comments about my work.

Due to these experiences, I reject much of our traditional teaching practices and attitudes. Have you ever been told in a job interview that you misspelled a word on your resume, and subsequently did not get the job? I have. It says more about them than about you. As I wondered whether they weren't able to see beyond the spelling error into how I think or what I could really do for them.

I am constantly reminded that I've misspelled a word in some important document. People think I am careless and sloppy or don't review my work, which is not correct in any way.

I still use the same techniques I learned in high school of rereading things multiple times. I even reread emails many times before sending them. Thank goodness for spellcheckers, but occasionally I slip up because the spellchecker changes the word.

Dyslexia did not immobilize me at work. In my career, I've taught middle and high school students, instructed teachers to use innovative techniques, was elected as president of the state science teachers' association, launched a startup organization, served on local and national boards of directors, wrote and received millions of dollars in federal grants, coauthored three books, and held the executive director position in three organizations (two at the state level and the other at the national level). I catalogue these positions not to boast, but to illustrate that learning challenges do not hinder your ability to succeed.

I have come to learn that my view of the world is different than others'. Psychologists also say people with dyslexia approach tasks with greater mindfulness and really think about what they are doing. People with dyslexia often innovate and experiment with procedures and processes to find new and better ways of doing things. Dyslexia may have made me more inclined for connected leadership.

I have become aware that I focus on processes, people, systems, and the future. I often look around the corner at what is not immediately apparent, rather than getting bogged down in the details of daily activities. I have found people and systems that can help me mitigate my language weaknesses. Recently I read an article that said when writing emails, you should try to use common language rather than sounding too formal. The article went on to suggest you could even misspell a word or two to make it seem like you are more concerned about connecting with the individual than the formality of language. I thought, "Wow, I have been doing that all along!"

Thinking differently is a positive trait in business. You may run into some obstacles, but it allows you to build resilience, flexibility, and creativity because of tactics you already employ just to get through the day. There are many skills you develop as you build ways to succeed.

Through my dyslexia, I developed empathy for others who were struggling, whether based on minority, gender, or economic status. You learn to appreciate people for what they can do rather than looking for what they can't. I believe this is key to finding the right people to help you advance projects or tasks, as well as for making decisions about who to work with and whether you can trust them. Those who focus on the end game are great collaborators, as they know where they are going. Getting there is part of the adventure.

Business as an Ecosystem

The challenges organizations face today are complex. Many of them we can't solve as single leaders. We must depend on other leaders and employees and hence collaborate. This book will help you understand how to navigate and succeed in the complex business ecosystem of the modern world.

Advanced digital technology has transformed the way businesses operate. It is already being used extensively in manufacturing, but in the future, with Industry 4.0 (the fourth industrial revolution), it will transform production too. With greater efficiencies, it will change traditional production relationships among suppliers, producers, and customers—as well as between humans and machines.

How will this impact our relationships and the way people and machines work together? People will still be critical. I hope that with Industry 4.0, companies, departments, functions, and capabilities will become much more cohesive as cross-company data-integration networks evolve and automation becomes more advanced.

Think about where and how we carry out work in business—it's an ecosystem of employees, customers, contractors, suppliers, distribution lines, and communications.

From a scientific perspective, an ecosystem is a complex set of interactions of living and non-living things that are critical for the survival of all parts of the system, living or otherwise.

For example, one natural ecosystem is a coastal saltwater marsh. The microscopic animals and plants that live in the marsh are critical for maintaining the plants and soils. The larger plants and animals support other animals, including interlopers such as birds that fly in and out. Birds leave waste behind, promoting plant growth and helping aerate the soil. The plants provide food for some organisms. Fish of all sorts depend on marshes to spawn and grow in, and for protection before they are released into the wide-open ocean full of other predators. All of these factors rely on one another to support themselves.

A business or a specific project within a business works much the same. At the microlevel, individuals and teams interact—whether they're seeking advice from one another, conducting product development, or selling to customers, their interactions are many.

There are support systems in a business ecosystem: IT, communication, security, and transportation might be needed, along with the approval or authority structures for making decisions so things move forward.

How many of these, if removed, would have a negative effect on a project's progress? If one of them is removed or fails, the system starts to break down, like a natural ecosystem. This happens all the time—a leader doesn't like an idea and tries to cut it off, someone misses a deadline and the production flow is disrupted, or a team member recruits others to be a barrier in a project. External factors can also disrupt the flow, such as transportation delays or if vital service workers go on strike.

Any number of internal or external factors can influence the success of a project. In a business ecosystem, there are both people concerns and systems concerns, and those can be internal or external to the organization. That's a lot to organize, and if something goes wrong, it can derail your entire project or even your business.

Effective collaboration can strengthen your business or project in order to keep it from breaking down when something unexpected happens. However, collaboration requires a strong purpose that will engage others to understand why this project or business is important. People are more willing to put in effort toward a compelling goal. You want the people involved to adequately promote and support others, knowing they're doing important work for the project, division, or company.

Our human need for connections and interactions with each other is an intrinsic part of the ecosystem because it motivates us to remain accountable and focused, and to work with others to create better outcomes.

When you think collaboratively, your perspective includes who, what, and how others are able to help you or your business. Often, we look inside our organizations and ask what capacities we have to accomplish a new product or project, then either hire or train people if the gaps are too large. This increases other internal and management costs. From an ecosystem perspective, it's better to ask, "What are the capacities and interactions that are critical and have a commitment to the product or project success?" Then look inside and outside the organization or team to fill the gaps.

The people or organizations who have a commitment are those who will find some benefit in working with you. Benefits might be producing something or providing a service that will make the product better, faster, or cheaper; obtaining greater visibility to their customers; or gaining expertise from you in exchange for assisting or collaborating. This type of collaboration creates shared accountability: if the product or project fails, they fail too. They need skin in the game. As in an ecosystem, all the players need to find a way to work together so everyone benefits. Otherwise the system collapses.

As a collaborative leader, your view of other people and organizations is different from the view of a directive leader, which gives you a benefit in thinking about complex efforts that require many people and diverse knowledge. While you may compete in some areas like a directive leader does, in others you collaborate. This behavior is often seen in ecosystems. An ecosystem is not a top-down system. Collaboration isn't either.

Nontraditional Leadership

Seeing differently is both helpful and necessary in our current and future workplaces. As an individual in the modern business ecosystem, it is impossible to separate all aspects of a problem into its parts, understand those individual parts, and put it back together and make it work. Understanding the pieces doesn't mean you understand how those pieces work together. Sometimes it is possible to understand how the pieces work together with complicated problems, but complex problems are becoming more common than complicated problems.

Complicated challenges and complex challenges are different. Complicated challenges are technical in nature and follow a linear process. Complex challenges are more creative in nature, meaning they can be messy, unstable, unpredictable, and multidimensional. They require strategic and innovative thinking as the right answer is not always apparent. Usually these problems take multiple people or organizations to solve because they are not linear.

Most leaders today grew up with the idea that you can simplify things by looking at the parts. When you reassemble the parts, you know how the whole works. You can blame this mindset on physics. Do you know the difference between Newtonian and quantum physics? In the Newtonian view, particles of an atom have predictable orbits that we can track. In quantum physics, it is extremely hard to predict where those particles will be and if you say, "They are here," they will have already moved. Sometimes they act as waves and other times as particles.

"The quantum world is weird," is a common refrain for scientists. Scientists are getting better at predicting quantum behavior, but when you try to measure its changes, its behavior remains weird. Quantum physics is a relatively new aspect of physics, conceived in the 1920s but still not well understood.

This is the type of dilemma that exists in the business world, where you may think you have a solution, but there are unexpected implications. There are just too many components and players for any one person or leader to solve the problems, just as scientists have not solved how quantum behavior works.

This is how it is with leadership. You know the players and what they may want, but at any time they may act unpredictably. They fit nicely in a chart, but to pin them down is tricky and hence it's useful to communicate often, listen, and connect them to one another so they listen to each other.

Another way to think about this is the difference between complex versus complicated problems. We have generally grown up in a mechanical or industrial world. People have been able to take things apart to understand them. Today a better analogy for how complex problems and business work is a biological one. Things interact at times in ways that are not well understood. And sometimes things change depending on the biological cycle.

Being the sole entrepreneur who wants to solve everything is not sustainable. What can you do to change the sole entrepreneur mindset? Simply find ways to work with others. Scientists have been doing this for centuries. As a leader, accept that others may know more than you and let them take the lead on aspects of the problem. If this sounds like connected leadership or collaboration, then you're already making progress. Seeing differently means solving problems in new ways.

Leaders must begin to address and use collaboration. Let's say you have a challenge you have worked on for a while, but you aren't making progress and there are two strong opposing viewpoints. Not uncommon, right?

This is like the Chinese finger puzzle. It is a child's toy. If you put your finger in one end and a friend puts their finger in the other end and you each try to pull your finger out, the puzzle tightens. The more the participants pull, the tighter the puzzle gets, increasing the pressure and trapping them both.

Many leaders are familiar with this tug-of-war of ideas. Two people have opposing viewpoints and instead of trying to work through a solution, a conflict begins. The way to resolve the Chinese finger puzzle is for both people to relax their fingers and push toward each other. This reduces the tension and the finger puzzle opens wide enough to withdraw your fingers.

If you apply this technique to people with opposing viewpoints, you get cooperation. Each person sets aside their position for a bit to better understand the other person's viewpoint. Then they can evaluate how they might move their idea toward the other's viewpoint and perhaps obtain an agreeable solution. New ideas and possible solutions can be generated when the mind is more open.

You can ask, "How do we meet the needs of each of the two positions without discarding one of them completely?" Just asking the question could help you to see new aspects to the problem. The barriers that slow decision-making are preconceived ideas, beliefs, or emotions, and they get us locked into our thinking and cause us to be unwilling to move. These can be thoughts such as "I need to win to show how smart I am," "It will advance my career if I have the right answer," or "I am angry at this other person and having the right answer will get back at them." These examples represent self-speak, which can take us offtrack and is focused on self rather than the team, company, or larger outcome. When confronted with a complex problem that has multiple dimensions, it takes cooperation to solve—a give and take of ideas.

Working with other people in a collaborative fashion works. Energy is generated among people who are focused on solving a common problem. A human connection is made. New ideas are generated. The process can move more quickly.

Collaboration is also hard to do. There are many reasons for this: people may have personal agendas; collaboration is not generally structurally encouraged in the workplace; everyone thinks differently so consensus is sometimes not quick or even possible; and

Western culture reveres individuality. Incentives are often individually based.

There are many books and articles written about collaboration and still it is a challenge for many. I hesitated to even use the word collaboration for this book as it comes with baggage. People think collaboration is for wimps who can't accomplish tasks alone, takes too long, is anticompetitive, or is a soft skill—and for some, it has links to gender bias.

There are other words related to collaboration such as networks, partnerships, cooperation, alliance, and incubators, which are popular now. With the interest in innovation, collaboration can be viewed as a catalyst for innovation.

Barry Oshry, President of Power + Systems, Inc., says multiple people working together is effective because they are able to "see others, get who they are and what is important to them, and [this] helps them move ahead in their worlds." The subtlety of collaborative leadership and its lack of a singular locus of control can make collaborations challenging in the context of traditional, directive leadership.

Many people struggle with the concept in collaborative leadership that the buck does not stop with the executive director or CEO. With today's complex and fast-moving world, one person can't make all the decisions. They can take the ultimate accountability, but the consequences of decisions are shared.

A singular focus on one person as the locus of control is in conflict with collaborative leadership. Empowering and engaging others spreads the credit and accountability. To not always be in the spotlight is to continually remind others that we want to accomplish a goal together and to support them with recognition. Of course there are times when decisions do need to be made by one person, and that will likely never change—but if everything is funneled through one person, then the leadership model is directive, not collaborative.

Working Together

Most leadership models emphasize the importance of working together toward the same goal or in the same direction. Effective collaboration is more complicated than it seems because the people and incentives involved in a project or business may not support the collaborative effort. Ultimately, you want to have multiple people working toward the same purpose. I sometimes refer to this as aligning the vectors. The vectors represent different people, teams, departments, divisions, or companies.

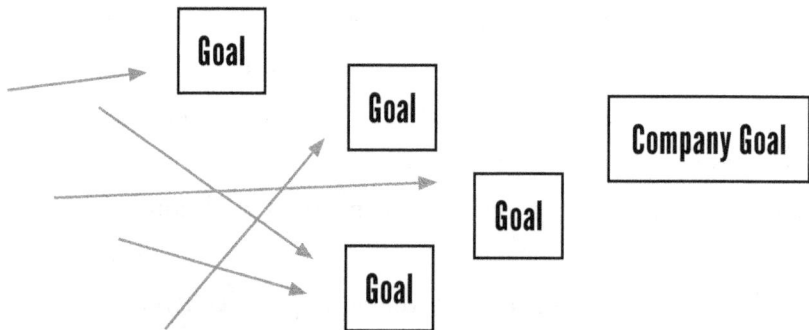

This diagram illustrates a situation where each person (vector) believes they are working together, but they aren't truly collaborating. Each of them is "winning" at *their* goal. For instance, the sales group is promoting and selling a product that is benefiting the company in terms of revenue. At the same time the engineering/ quality group has found some defects and have developed a fix. The new version of the product is more expensive, and the sales group is having trouble selling it, so they revert to the earlier version. They are hitting their sales goal. The engineering group has done their work to develop the better version, hence they accomplished their goal. Together these two ends are not the best for the company or their clients.

The same thing can happen with a team when there is competition among the members. Competition results in one or more members hiding information, not sharing what they are learning from customers, or talking to the leader about their plans rather than the team so they can be more successful at the expenses of others on the team. This is the worst case: people end up working against each other within a company, lowering both revenue and engagement.

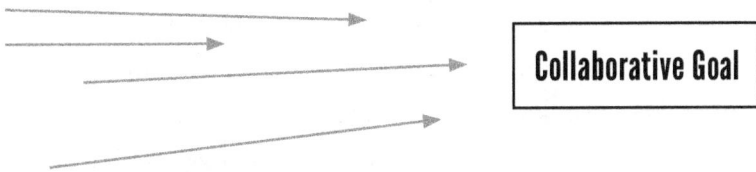

Collaborative Goal

When the vectors or groups are aligned and working toward a single goal, they have purposeful coordination even though they may be doing separate work. They can come from different places, move at different rates, and still achieve the same goal.

An example is a company that has developed a product that will enhance another healthcare product. It reduces the contamination of blood in transfusions and results in better health outcomes for patients. The benefit to patients is only realized if the company who makes the original healthcare product is willing to use this add-on. They have to agree that perhaps some short-term loss in revenue will show better outcomes for patients and, in the long run, more sales and better revenue. If the two companies collaborate to produce the combined product, they both benefit.

Initially, collaboration may seem to be more arduous and involved than a more direct approach to leadership. Don't let this discourage you—once the conditions are in place, more options become available, employees have a stronger purpose, and actions are better coordinated.

So what does this kind of collaboration look like in a business environment? Here's an example:

A communications services company was baffled when only 65 percent of customers got a working connection when they first attempted to use a premium fiberoptic product. The sales, back office, operations, and logistic teams all were hearing positive feedback. On closer inspection, an executive discovered the field engineers were under pressure to meet new orders and had cut down on the time they spent with customers during installation. Less was known about the customers' needs and problems. Meanwhile, back-office staff were struggling to cope with incomplete and often incorrect orders submitted by the sales team. The sales, marketing, and field engineers weren't addressing all they had control over and deflected some problems to other people. Meeting the needs of customers was not a part of individual or functional performance targets. The collaboration was weak and incentives were misaligned and as a result, the potential breakthrough was not realized.

To improve this situation, the company established cross-functional teams charged with controlling the installation process from initial order to after-sales service. The impact was tangible, as working connections increased to over 80 percent from the earlier 65 percent, customer satisfaction was up, and the number of call requests for help dropped by one-third in the first six weeks after installation.

The Power of Collaborative Thinking

How many arguments have begun because another person says something that seems contrary or even offensive to your perception of a situation? In order to have a productive conversation, at least one of the participants must strive to understand the other person's viewpoint. This diversion from a direct confrontation, which is what we naturally tend to do, can open the other person's thinking. It is even better if both can have an open mind. Once some understanding occurs, there are specific tactics you can use to try to modify your opinion or encourage the other person to reevaluate their position.

Neuroscientists have learned remarkable things about the human brain. For example, people can deeply affect one another with their words, tone, and how they approach one another. The old adage about sticks and stones and words isn't true—words do hurt. If we know more about how we relate to each other, particularly as we increase our dependence on technology for communication, we can become more effective leaders. Humans crave face-to-face connections, which are not yet duplicated by technology. Thinking collaboratively means involving others and reducing the isolation of the individual. That requires learning how others think.

> **Collaborative thinking is the ability to think with others about solving the problem at hand.**

We live in a complex world, a VUCA world (volatile, uncertain, complex, and ambiguous), which requires thinking in ways that are different. Many decisions benefit from having more than one person thinking it through. Let's take a look at a couple of different mindsets and how they approach problems:

A market-share mindset is one defined by scarcity or shortage of resources. The idea is "I have it and you don't." According to Gardner and Matvaik in their *Harvard Business Review* article, in times of anxiety, such as in a crisis, people become more risk-averse and are less likely to seek a wide range of ideas. The market-share mindset makes it fairly easy to break problems down into a sequence or its parts and reason through them because of the limited resources. It is a bifurcated way of thinking: your gain is someone else's loss. A leader ascends to an executive level through other's losses. Success here is measured in what is gained and not in what is lost.

Contrary to this view is a mind-share mindset. This idea was introduced by a former U.S. IKEA CEO, Anders Dahlvig. He believed wealth is created and carried by *ideas and relationships* more than through transactions. With this mindset, the measure of success is not a physical *thing*—currency, property, or an object. Success is not extrinsic. The mind-share mindset is intrinsic because it places value on ideas and relationships. An idea or relationship is not something you trade (although an exception could be patents). It promotes better connections with people and sharing of ideas. Ultimately, this mindset will help us gain because we'll learn from each other and everyone will grow. The ability to communicate well and learn how others think is a valuable skill in a culture with a mind-share mindset.

The power of collaborative thinking is the power of influencing others through ideas. The strength of ideas and those people who can think flexibly will be the most influential. Daniel Pink writes in *A Whole New Mind* that most of us have been educated with a market-share mindset and our skills in communication and problem-solving are based in the winning outcome. Why do you think the notion of win-win was so radical when Steven Covey first raised it in his book *The Seven Habits of Highly Successful People* in 1989? And the book is still relevant today. A leader's capacity to bridge differences hasn't evolved as fast as the changing world around us, which is much more complex.

The Art of Inquiry

How do you learn to think differently? Step out of your current context and be curious. The way I have learned to do this is through the art of inquiry. You can build your skill by asking questions. Think through your questions before speaking, study questioning, and observe others. Watch leaders who you admire and see how often they ask questions rather than making suggestions or giving directions.

Inquiry is critical when a conversation seems to be headed toward an argument. If you start asking questions instead of trying to push harder on your point, you can help the other person think through their position and perhaps change it. You open up their thinking by helping them see there is more than one way to address or see the problem. When they're defending their position, they are in the advocate stance, which is a one-way method of communication.

If you take an inquiry stance, which is a form of two-way communication, they will have to *engage* rather than *tell*. This allows you more flexibility to learn, react, adjust, and see things differently.

Consider a discussion about job performance. The employee you are talking with starts to dispute their actions and role on a team. As their tone changes, stop and ask questions such as the following: "What does good communication on an effective team look like? How are people on the team working through problems? Do you exhibit those characteristics on the team? What are some things you can do to enhance the team's abilities to solve problems? What is your role as a team member in helping make those things happen?"

As you ask questions, you can guide the person back to their behaviors. Ask, "Do you exhibit those behaviors you just listed?" Then move to a positive question: "What can you do to exhibit those behaviors?"

These questions raise the conversation up a level. You take a conversation heading for conflict about the details into a discussion about bigger issues.

> **Conflict can be more easily resolved by asking questions to reinforce the goal and directing focus away from the details.**

Go up a level until you can get an agreement on the purpose and global actions that should happen. Then move back down into the detail once you define where you are going or what is most effective. Stay up there until you get agreement.

In an article called "The Art of Inquiry," Dave Coffaro, principal of Strategic Advisory Consulting Group, presents a framework for using inquiry to solve complex problems in a collaborative environment. It requires a deductive position, which means you learn about the bigger picture through the context of the situation. Think of it as a funnel. You begin at the top, the widest part of the funnel, and seek to understand the specific situation in the context of the problem.

Here are some example questions:

1. What is the purpose of this project?

2. Why was leadership willing to commit to this project?

3. What does success look like?

4. How does this project leverage our competencies as an organization?

5. Who else in the company could offer insight into the situation or type of work?

Next, you begin to move down the funnel by listening to the types of questions asked by others. Before it seems like you are getting to a final idea, stop and add this question: What question have we not asked and answered?

The conversation can become wider or more focused depending on the level of agreement. Allow time to do this. Distill the answers and repeat them to the person or team to ensure you understand. If used well, this technique can build solutions, form new relationships, and encourage anyone outside the organization to feel they have input.

Leaders need to find ways to connect people and to help them apply their skills and knowledge so the participants feel empowered and appreciated. Working through complex problems with people and organizations can build a renewed sense of respect because it reveals talents. Each person brings something unique to the problem-solving process.

Foster Collaborative Intelligence

A leader needs to recognize the context of the conversation, especially when matters are outside your control or the control of your company, like in an external partnership. Leaders have more control when they understand the company's context, and they can add value by bringing that into the conversation. If resources are slim, people behave differently than when everyone has what they want. Some people become more intelligent and capable when they know things are tight. Liz Wiseman says about collaboration, "Eighty people can either operate with the productivity of fifty or they can operate as though they were five hundred." (Wiseman, 2017) People are more likely to work together when resources are slim. If there is a tug-of-war around budgets, it is a good time to stop and revisit the assumptions people are making. Who else might be helpful in making the decision, including outside expertise? How you process ideas to foster "collaborative intelligence" can make a difference.

As a start to developing your collaborative intelligence, you can do the following:

- ▶ Observe a leader whom you admire and see what kind of questions they ask and when they ask them.

- ▶ Notice if authority is given to others and how it is done.

- ▶ Observe others in your typical team meetings and see how often they ask questions rather than talk. Record the behaviors.

As you are observing and learning from others, is the leader or team asking and learning, or are they advocating? The difference is key to know how far you will have to go to build a collaborative team.

James Surowiecki wrote about collaborative intelligence in his book *The Wisdom of Crowds*. He calls it *collective* intelligence. Four conditions are needed for it to grow and develop:

- ▶ Diverse opinions to avoid group thinking

- ▶ Independent thinking without judgment so everyone is able to express their opinion

- ▶ Decentralization of problem-solving

- ▶ A way to collect results

I will discuss each of these four conditions as we progress through the book.

Because I accepted my learning disability as my normal and worked to develop and expand my strengths of seeing the big picture, pulling pieces together and synthesizing ideas, being diplomatic, and helping others achieve and succeed, I moved to new leadership roles. I needed other people. My attitude was one of a growth mindset rather than accepting my disability as static or something that would hold me back.

Learn to Think Differently

How do you begin to think differently, if it doesn't come naturally?

Psychologist and writer Maria Konnikova, in her book *Mastermind: How to Think Like Sherlock Holmes*, writes: "To observe, you must learn to separate situation from interpretation, yourself from what you are seeing."

She suggests if you are trying to understand a situation with more clarity, you should describe the situation or problem to someone else, or describe it in writing. The process of articulating a problem in the absence of having the pressure of a live, interactive conversation seems to help the mind think in different ways.

I apply this technique to communication and leadership by planning first alone and then with others. Sometimes it is good to pause. Often, I will not engage right away with someone if a conflict is rising or when developing some new ideas. I will pick the conversation up later to give myself some time to think it through. I consider how they may be thinking about the concept and perhaps talk with other people about their perspective before reengaging. This provides me with options to manage the conversation. I also often write out the sequence of a project or organizational strategy, including all sorts of opportunities and tangential people, products, and organizations.

Adam Brandenburger also addresses this technique in his 2019 *Harvard Business Review* article "To Change the Way You Think, Change the Way You See." If you take a step back and look wider, you will see what is in front of you and that there is much more to an issue than the individual players or parts. This allows you to look for patterns and behaviors and assess who is trying to move things forward and who is not. You can also ask, "Does this problem show up in other contexts?" and "What would someone with a naïve viewpoint see in this problem?" These approaches help the mind unlock from a singular focus to one that is more open and help you become a strategic leader.

Consider your situation from the perspective of what you *can* control. This idea is articulated well in Steve and Jill Morris's book *Leadership Simple: Leading People to Lead Themselves*. You only have control over yourself and your behaviors. While this may seem like it shrinks the world, this concept can be valuable as it helps you understand what *others* have control over, which allows you to identify sources of needed expertise and develop a strategy to work with them.

The antithesis of this mindset is a blame mindset where you place blame on others or systems you have no control over. By doing so, you give away your influence. You allow others to dictate what you can do. For example, take a manager who is leading an ineffective team and can't figure the problem out. They blame the team and don't take any action to change the situation. The leader has enabled the team to be ineffective. By not taking action, the leader has given their influence away.

To exert your influence, develop strategies to help change the situation. If asked, the team might suggest an agenda in advance, have a timekeeper and topic manager to stay on topic, or volunteer to run part of the meeting. These are actions that might improve the way the team works. And there are many others. Notice all of these things are in the team members' and the leader's control. A leader is not powerless and team members aren't powerless either, just because they don't have the positional authority. Both parties still have control of their behavior.

A local independent radio station I listen to occasionally runs an advertisement with the tagline "Be a nerd, not a part of the herd." I love this, because the implication is your life is up to you and you choose it. Will you embrace thinking differently or shy away and conform?

A question I often use to end work sessions with teams is from *The Accidental CEO* by Thomas Voccola. The goal is to get team members to reflect on the day and their role on the team. "Will you choose to be a part of designing the future of this company, or are you just reacting to it?"

The Role of Competition

It's not bad to be competitive. You can have competitive efforts within a collaboration, and sometimes the overall strategy of a collaboration is to be competitive within the marketplace. The most destructive competition is between individuals and sometimes teams.

Developing an attitude of acting is necessary for collaboration because often a single person isn't saying what to do. Actions can be taken in many places by many people and sometimes without the full knowledge of everyone involved. It does require understanding the collaborative goal and working toward that goal.

Be attentive to the influence others have on a group or company and how that affects the group.

Diversity

I started this chapter talking about how I think about the world. To return to this idea, I am a strong believer in diversity of thought. What I mean by diversity is variation in expertise, background, experience, and skills. Cultural diversity often refers to race and background. A study conducted by Amir Goldberg from Stanford University looked at diversity of interpersonal and intrapersonal connections. Interpersonal connection, even with culturally diverse groups, detracts from performance while intrapersonal diversity (thinking differently) increases it. Groups can be formed with cultural differences, but effort has to be made to develop purpose or support for working together. Groups should have diverse ideas, thinking (which can come from cultural diversity but not always), and efforts to support their working together to problem-solve.

Another study, conducted at Google and called Project Aristotle, found that teams with only a few star players often perform better than teams with all star players. This seems counterintuitive. Everyone wants to have the best people, the A-players. However, sports teams with lots of stars often struggle and are beaten by teams of lesser-known players. Why is that? The stars are generally more focused on their own performance and ultimately will compete with each other on the same team for prominence and recognition. They act as individuals and sometimes discourage dissent or equal speaking time. Their thinking is not pushed by new ideas, as they believe they already have all the answers or skill. The teams with a mixture of players found they had more sensitivity for each other's ideas. They were more willing to hear each other out. They were skilled at intuiting how others felt based on things such as tone of voice, expressions, and other nonverbal cues. If this factor exists on any team, they will be more successful (Duhigg and Graham). When selecting the people for a team, think about looking for people with diverse ideas, talents, experiences, social sensitivity, and a desire to succeed.

Diversity in this case is about how people think and the different approaches they take to solving problems. Diverse thinking comes with people from different backgrounds, experiences, and opportunities. Diversity of thought does not always come with diversity in attributes we can see or hear, such as race or language differences, but these attributes certainly promote it.

Today we can identify how people think and work with a range of assessment tools. A useful activity is to identify behaviors and motivations of team members, post them somewhere, and let the team review them. They can look for similarities, differences, and areas of conflict or synergy. I like to use the assessments offered by TTI Success Insights (Target Training International Success Insights). What is most important in any assessment tool is its validity and the research supporting it, and whether it is the right assessment for what you want to address. The most popular assessment is not a good choice if it doesn't fit your purpose.

A team of engineers might think very differently from a team of marketers, and if either is homogenous, there can be potential problems. Some simple examples might include whether they are detail oriented or make quick decisions without all the information. The detail-oriented people are helpful in idea refinement and project design and testing. The people who make quick decisions are helpful in idea generation, scaling, and marketing. These differences are important and if recognized on a team, the individuals' strengths can be incorporated in problem-solving work.

If a team has all one type of thinker, group thinking can happen very quickly. One way to reduce this is outlined by something called the group think theory (Art Markman, *Harvard Business Review*, 2015). Try letting individuals think separately first. They think differently about a problem if they work alone. When a group is together, particularly one that works together regularly, they tend to think alike. They converge on a common solution often too quickly.

There may be certain kinds of work or problems that some people are better at while others are better at being supportive of that activity. Aligning those differences or similarities for certain tasks can rocket a team forward and provide better results than the same team members all trying to complete the tasks themselves.

Seeing problems, ideas, and solutions differently can be slow going, but once the team understands each other, they can adapt and incorporate team members in ways that are beneficial and move more quickly. Extrapolate this method to other teams, departments, or divisions in a company, and even to the hierarchy of an organization, and it will become easier to see why some ideas never go anywhere and others do. Without the understanding of why people think the way they do, decisions are often made by those with experience rather than by the best thinkers for a particular problem.

By going further out to external subcontractors, remote workers, partners, alliances, suppliers, boards, and customers, all of which are critical in a business ecosystem, you can see that things can get complex. It is hard to control external players, so understanding why they do what they do is extremely helpful. It is not possible to assess all these constituencies in a business ecosystem, but if the members of a team are fluent with the psychology of behaviors and motivators, they can adapt themselves to be more flexible and assist others to be more effective with social sensitivity.

Reflection

There are many things you can do to learn how others think. Below are some ways to explore the thinking and behaviors of others.

1. Use a psychological assessment to determine your team's behavioral patterns and motivations. Look for one that has research behind it and can provide you with some ideas to help the individual with communication and what they might look for in a workplace.

2. Spend time identifying the problem or challenge you want to solve. Then outline the types of skills and behaviors that could be helpful in solving it, and think about whether you need to expand beyond your normal team members to assemble an effective team.

3. Develop a team that utilizes each others' strengths so they all add value.

    ▶ Assess them and map their results.

    ▶ What behaviors are predominant in the group?

    ▶ What kind of thinking is the go-to for the team?

    ▶ What are the team's weaknesses or things they avoid?

    ▶ What behaviors come out when your team is worried, stressed, or rushed?

    ▶ Where is the support they may need and how can you access it?

4. In hiring or selecting team members, ask some probing questions to determine their work patterns or experiences.

    ▶ Tell me about a time when you were fully engaged.

    ▶ What were the conditions that allowed that to happen?

▸ In your current work situation, what factors energize you and make you want to be a part of the team?

▸ When someone challenges you, how do you respond?

▸ What specifically annoys or frustrates you the most about other people?

▸ What could be driving you to act this way?

▸ Does this relate to a weakness that you or they have?

▸ How can you learn from them?

▸ How could you create a partnership where we support each other's weaknesses?

2

The Model

As the first lone cyclist reaches the peak of the Col du Galibier, an elevation of 2,642 meters in the southern region of the French Dauphiné Alps, the crowds cheer. This is the eighth highest paved road in the Alps, and the highest point of the Tour de France. The cyclist is recognized for their achievement and receives points toward the overall grueling two-week Tour de France race. To the casual watcher of bike races, this is an amazing feat, apparently done alone. To the cycling enthusiast it is an amazing feat too, but they know the cyclist did not achieve this climb alone.

Cycling is a team sport where individuals are supported in order for their expertise to shine. Individuals *and* teams win in the Tour de France. Because the team win is so important, there are roles for cycling team members. There are the climbers, time trialists, all-around riders, and sprinters. Each plays a role in the team's success and supports others when their strength is needed. For example, during a long, flat race, the sprinters can ride behind their team members until the last few miles. They are more rested and are more able to sprint to the first place to get individual and team points. There are domestiques, or support riders, a term for workers on a team. These riders are unlikely to win any part of the race, but without them the "stars" have a hard time winning. Sometimes these supporters work so hard they end up dropping from the race due to exhaustion from helping the star climb more easily. These roles are laid out in a plan developed long before the race. The plan is continuously being evaluated as the racers change position and in response to the type of race that is presented each day over the two-week series.

Scientists now regularly collaborate with other scientists from different disciplines. Biologists and physicists or chemists and geologists, for example—sometimes there are three different disciplines working together. By working together, sharing data and expertise, they learn as individuals and as a team.

The advantage of different types of expertise is pretty evident for these people. This type of mix is not that common in business. The barriers to effective teams are things such as people chosen because of their title, for culture fit, or because they support an idea. The team members are similar in what they do even if they represent different disciplines. Cross-functional teams are less common. Team members are typically not selected because of a "weakness" they can add to a team.

However, incubator teams are becoming more common. Within a company, these teams are often composed of members from different areas working to solve a particular problem. These teams are usually short-term collaborations. They are formed and then disbanded, and a new team is formed to examine a new challenge. Experiments like these, if done well, can provide a valuable boost to your organization, revenue, and culture. This example of collaboration is much more like the examples from a cycling or science team because it moves people around or selects people to work on new outcomes.

Collaboration takes purposeful design and support. In this chapter, you'll learn the model for connected and collaborative leadership that will allow you to implement these strategies in your own team or business. The model goes through five steps that outline my recommendations for setting up and sustaining collaboration.

The concept for this model is based on my own experience and many other people's work. Collaboration is not new, but I have not found a model that matches my experiences or research. There are lists of attributes and characteristics of effective collaborative people, groups, or organizations, but none address what I believe to be one of the most important aspects: cultivating *attention*.

The Model

I developed a visualization of a model to illustrate how collaboration works in a business ecosystem. This chapter will explain the important aspects of collaboration so you can execute it internally within a team or business, or externally with business partnerships.

At first glance, this model makes the aspects of collaboration seem simple. You may even say to yourself, "I already do that." This is one of the biggest challenges with collaboration: everyone knows something about it, but enacting it is hard.

The most important aspect of collaboration is the interaction among the people involved.

This model places value on the people involved. It is not the only way to work with others, but it can help develop and achieve collaborative efforts. The purpose of the model is to provide a tool for leaders as they guide their organizations. Leaders can use this model to develop strategies to solve complex problems.

This chapter will give you an overview of the components of the model and how they work together, and the following chapters will go into more detail about each component.

As you go through this chapter, keep in mind that the quality of the interaction between the parts of the model is most important. This is key in effective connected leadership, because it is where you find the difference between truly collaborating and just working together. Two people working together may or may not be collaborating. Think about the people on your team or in your organization. Are they working for themselves or the team? Are they trying to advance their own goals at the expense of others or the company? Do they take on others' work or just focus on their own? Just because people are in the same room does not mean they are collaborating.

The Four Components

Ecosystem

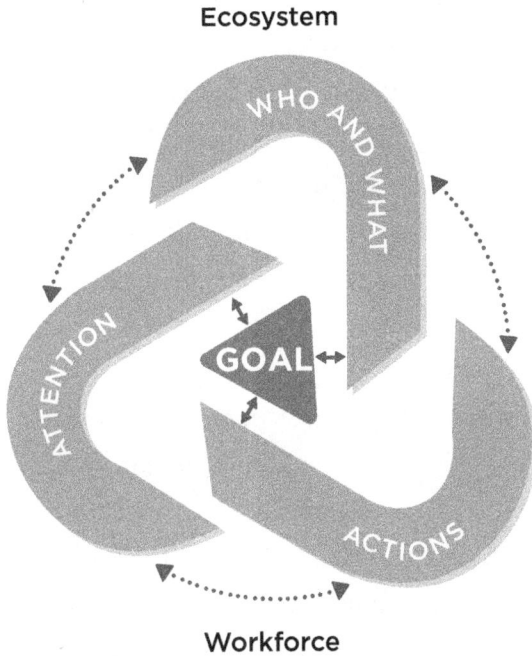

Workforce

Goal: Vision and Purpose

Who and What: People, Roles, Infrastructure

Actions: Communications, Capacities, Capabilities, Systems, Commitment

Attention: Engagement, Roles, Monitoring, Problems, Progress, Celebration

This model has four aspects: clarifying the goal, carefully selecting the people involved, carrying out actions, and cultivating attention. Within these aspects are a number of principles, and hence there may not be a clear sequence for every situation. What makes this model effective is the interaction of people with the situation at hand, and these principles can act as a mirror to cultivate attention and build focus and momentum.

1. Clarify the Goal

The goal is the most critical part of any collaboration as it provides the guiding star or vision. Whatever you are trying to accomplish with your project or business, it needs to be big enough to resonate with people's values or motivations (intrinsic), rather than focusing on things (extrinsic) or the processes (systemic). You might think of a large goal as a mission or vision. This works for organizations. For departments or teams within an organization, it is helpful to create a goal that resonates with team members and leads to the organizational goal.

To accomplish a larger goal, there are often smaller goals to complete on the way. Some examples might be creating logistics systems to track the production and transportation of a product, creating designs that will be applied to the development of a new facility, or gaining the support necessary for you to reach your goal. Breaking apart the larger goal into tasks requires you to identify the right people, organizations, or skills needed to achieve the smaller and larger goals.

Organizations that push ahead without spending enough time developing and communicating their goals may find they are not prepared for the obstacles ahead.

Appealing to people with a sense of purpose in working toward a goal and their role in accomplishing that goal is more effective than other approaches of encouragement or accountability systems. It is also effective team leadership.

Here are a couple of examples of larger organizational goals or missions that create a greater sense of purpose for team members.

Zappos' mission is to "provide the best customer service possible. Deliver WOW through service." This helps their employees think of their work as serving people rather than selling shoes.

LinkedIn's mission is "to connect the world's professionals to make them more productive and successful." Even though the company is digital, their mission provides context: who and why.

These examples include a context that is meaningful, connects to people, provides something to measure, and allows for more specific goals and tasks to be spelled out to accomplish them. How do Zappos' employees serve people? By selling shoes. Remember, it is people who do the work, and they have to be inspired or committed to the work to have strong engagement. These goals allow flexibility but still allow accountability to be built in.

2. Carefully Select the People Involved and Their Roles (Who and What)

The second major component of this model is the who: the individuals, teams, departments, organizations, partners, suppliers, contractors, and advisors, and the roles they will play. Identifying the right people or organizations with the skills and capabilities to move forward is key. If you do not have the requisite skills within your team or organization, go outside your organization to find them or train people already within your organization.

The process of choosing team members is constantly in flux and is not something to progress through too quickly. The skills and responsibilities likely will change, sometimes rapidly.

The people involved need to receive regular and consistent messages and support. It's easy to relax or regress if not constantly reminded of your role and the impact you have on achieving the goal. Andy Johnson, in his book *Pushing Back Entropy*, calls this "slacking entropy." Entropy is a word describing the natural world's tendency to move to a lower-energy state when left alone. Think of it as "going downhill." A leader's job is to help people and teams to keep going up the hill with support, appreciation, and acknowledgment for what they are doing to meet the goal.

Several recent studies by Google, ADP (Automatic Data Processing, Inc.), and Gallup have found that when people in teams are engaged, they are more productive, more creative, and happier. Team members need to understand what their role is in accomplishing the larger goal and that goal has to be challenging and purposeful. It also is great if it makes the world a better place. In business, people often act based on accountabilities, and targets are measured against them. These are written as tasks to be accomplished and the employee doesn't understand their role in reaching the goal or how the tasks are helping to achieve it.

Getting the right people could look like the following:

1. Identify what capacities are needed to complete the task.

2. Identify strategies and tactics, define dimensions of the work, and determine the capabilities needed.

3. Identify the people and systems that will be impacted or are needed to complete the task

Notice the people come after the capacities, strategies, and tactics are established. Don't form the team first to determine these things.

3. Carry Out the Plan (Actions)

One of the greatest strengths of the human brain is imagination. We can develop ideas and plans of all sorts. A historical fault for leaders is when they come up with a grand plan and then tell their employees to carry it out. Have you ever been told, "Just figure it out," or "You have control of this," only to find out later that the leader had another idea about what should happen? Many times, the solutions developed are not what the leader intended.

Employees do not know what is in the leader's mind and it can become a guessing game.

In the previous aspect of the model, people were selected and roles were assigned. Now it's time to follow through on those roles. If the roles are not clear enough, spend more time on them. Strong project management skills are helpful here.

Define the actions necessary to achieve the goal:

1. Describe roles and responsibilities clearly.

2. Match the capabilities of the people, teams, or organizations to the roles and responsibilities.

3. Place authority in capable hands—not all at the top.

4. Coordinate systems and action steps.

5. Review commitments through examining benefits and risks.

As an example, let's use a customer service center's goal "to provide solutions to customers' problems so they become remedies for their lives." What would the actions for this goal look like at this point in the process? Here are some thoughts. Though perhaps simplistic, I hope they give you a sense of what I mean:

1. Specify which people will take the calls from U.S. or international clients.

2. Ensure that when a call comes in, the employee has the information and resources to solve the problem. Organize them in teams so when not talking with customers, they can discuss past problems and solutions and develop the best options for potential problems.

3. Support the development of the employees to be empathic and understanding so they can better help customers.

4. Keep track by entering each call's problems and solutions for further analysis about what approaches work well.

5. Ensure informational resources are kept up to date and allowed to expand as the employees learn and find solutions.

6. Build in a feedback system for employees to talk informally about problems they are having and solutions without worrying about being evaluated. This feedback is for improvement, not evaluation.

4. Cultivate Attention

In collaboration and connected leadership, attention has several roles: accountability, problem identification, talent identification, and recognition. Attention from the leader and from team members allows you to keep a collaboration moving forward in the right direction and hold team members accountable based on expectations and authority.

Accountability for teams is too often focused on existing structures that have some negative connotations, such as performance evaluation or KPIs (key performance indicators), so keep looking. There are other ways to check on people and processes. For example, just regularly sharing information is a way of practicing attention because it provides an opportunity to think and comment. This is a type of accountability. Attention, as a component of the model for collaboration, is an ongoing determination of next steps.

We should be honest with ourselves that we evaluate people all the time. Waiting for an annual performance evaluation is not fair or helpful to an employee. Team meetings can function better if they are problem-identification sessions and not just problem-solving sessions and updates. People are more attentive if they have something to do with an idea rather than just listening. A team mantra should be "Bring problems!" This strategy builds attention and opportunities for thinking and creating action. As a leader, meetings like this allow you to observe the level of engagement, the nature of the problems, and the amount of progress that is being made in a more realistic way.

The attention component also requires recognition in two ways:

1. The recognition of a problem or a need for help. Your culture should be open and team members should be able to bring problems forward without worrying about being evaluated. In fact, making a problem-solving list could be a positive addition to meetings.

2. The celebration or recognition of a success. Some people like a celebration and others prefer recognition. We all appreciate when our work is seen and appreciated by others, particularly the leader.

What might team recognition look like on a customer service team with the goal "to provide solutions to customers' problems so they become remedies for their lives"? Outline who will work on this goal and their roles and actions. Build in systems to pay attention to what the team is learning and accomplishing toward this goal.

The leader of the team can create checkpoints for the team to continue to learn and adapt as their customers call. I am a proponent of more frequent and shorter check-ins rather than longer team meetings. For each meeting, problems can be shared and discussed and then the actions reviewed at the next check-in. A simple method often suggested is asking three questions:

1. What are you working on?

2. Do you have what you need to work on it?

3. What help can I provide?

The regular review should include some way to measure when a goal has been accomplished or not. It could be a simple scale of one to five. Give a five if they are making easy successes, and a one if they are spinning their wheels. Then over time, see if they ask for help or seek others. If so, increase the value. This is a measure of progress, not outcome. How well are they working day to day? In some cases, the problem they are trying to solve might be too hard. Then a reevaluation is needed as well as adjustments in scope and perhaps people. This is better done earlier in the process than months after it has started.

The measurement allows the team to assess how well they are solving problems. The leader can track results and provide feedback to the team in a weekly or monthly summary. The leader receives the information in real time, which creates accountability.

The leader and the team can determine how to recognize and celebrate milestones and successes. By allowing the team to give input and even recognition, it shifts decision-making from the leader to the team members and allows for their investment. The leader leads and facilitates the group.

Using the Model

We've now covered the four areas that are the essence of the model. They can interact in a sequence: the goal is always first, followed by people, actions, and finally attention. This sequence is important when starting out. However, once in a collaborative work environment, the aspects of the model should be addressed as needed rather than in sequence. The goal is the least likely to change, but it can as conditions change.

In collaborative work, there are multiple interactions between and across aspects. This is how connected leadership plays a helpful role. The interactions continue to happen throughout the process but not necessarily in the same ways. Having multiple leaders allows for faster decision-making and shared responsibility, which creates accountability. Once a system is set in motion, it may be difficult to carry out certain aspects in the same way because the rules or context might have changed, or the people are moving faster or slower than expected. The interactions or aspects of the model will need to adapt.

To implement this model, begin with the end in mind. Determine what is the ultimate goal you want to achieve and work backwards.

Step 1. Clarify the Goal

Think about the final outcome you want to achieve. Here are some questions that can help:

- ▶ What is your purpose?

- ▶ What will be different, or changed, if you succeed?

- ▶ What is the problem you are trying to solve?

- ▶ What question have we not asked yet?

- ▶ How will people talk about the product or service after they use it?

- ▶ What is the legacy of the product, service, or company? How will it be remembered?

Step 2. Carefully Select the People

Begin planning and considering what resource capacity you have.

- ▶ What human capacity do we have, and is it enough or do we need other people?

- ▶ What are the financial, equipment, and material resources we will need, and do we have the ability to access enough of them?

- ▸ Are there partners or other companies that would make this even better?

- ▸ When does this have to be done?

- ▸ What external and internal regulations or standards will we have to meet to achieve our goal?

- ▸ Who knows about these regulations or standards?

Step 3. Carry Out Actions

Begin with the plan and develop the milestones for completing the plan.

- ▸ What is the plan and what is missing?

- ▸ What will people need?

- ▸ Are the milestones we set doable and if not, what is missing?

- ▸ How will we know when the work is done?

- ▸ What are the reporting structures and are they too complex or too simplistic?

Step 4. Cultivate Attention

This is the accountability aspect of the model.

- ▸ What can we measure to know we are making progress? And what shouldn't we measure?

- ▸ What do we need to measure that will give us immediate feedback and allow for quicker adjustments?

▶ Can we measure primary indicator milestones that tell if we are on track, intermediate indicators, and result milestones?

▶ Who will collect, analyze, and share the information we gather?

▶ How often do we review what we measure to help us stay on track?

▶ How and when do we acknowledge and celebrate the progress we are making?

Use these steps as a roadmap to set up your collaboration. The model is iterative and not linear. Once the initiative has begun and the parts are moving, the steps will have to be occasionally reworked or reviewed. You can think of this as refreshing the initiative.

The Results

The answer to the question "What will be your or your company's legacy?" can create a stark image of the importance of collaboration. Collaborative efforts create greater and potentially longer-lasting impacts, with employees more engaged. More people or organizations working toward a common end creates value across an ecosystem.

In a collaborative environment, leaders spend more time thinking about future direction, strategy, and advancing the team or company. They are not tied to leading every step as there are other leaders. Team members are invested and accountable, which allows a leader to observe and lead on a broader scale. Leaders are still involved in convening, carrying out planning, cultivating accountability, nurturing needs, and sometimes refreshing.

The team members or companies share the work more broadly. Typically, a project doesn't reach much further than the team that works on it. In a collaborative environment, it will likely extend to many more people. Team members become more engaged and talk about their work with others. They become more productive.

Finally, new ways to measure activity and outcomes can come from collaborations. If you want to determine what is important, sales numbers by individual may not be the best measure. Measuring sales by group as well as new and returning customers is an intermediate measure. The ultimate goal might be the satisfaction of customers, and that is a meaningful metric.

The benefits of collaboration are worth the effort put into creating collaboration in the beginning. Reflect on the work you do and answer this question: Do you want to participate in the design of the future of the company (or team), or do you just want to react to it?

> **Collaboration provides an opportunity to design a different future.**

A question that is asked when evaluating whether this model will help a whole company is this: Can it be used to "fix" the culture in a company? Or perhaps more specifically, if employees are not very engaged can this help? The short answer is yes, of course, while the reality is there are many conditions that would need to be in place and others removed. It must start at the top of the organization with supportive, collaborative leadership.

Changing a company's culture is a long process. My suggestion is to assess the problem first. An effective diagnosis is important to target the best place to start and at what scale. Proposing a solution or place to start before really knowing the context and constraints is throwing money at a problem without knowing if it is even the right problem. Spend time identifying the problem. Then assess the people and learn about them and what they might be able to contribute.

Some problems you may see in a non-collaborative company include employees waiting to be told what to do or how to act, competition among team members who are looking for an advance, overworked employees who are afraid to ask questions, or disengaged employees who see their job as just a job. A collaborative style of leadership begins with the purpose (the first part of the model). Spend a good deal of time here.

The next step will require more cooperation by individuals. Starting with the leadership team is helpful as they begin removing barriers, encouraging their teams to become more collaborative, and establishing new leaders. They will have to do this for some time, monitor their leaders' and teams' behavior, and not reward competition, holding information back, group think, biases, or individual recognition above the support for the team. The CEO must do this with the leadership team as well. The leadership team will need to be accountable for collaborative behavior throughout the organization.

Like stress, we don't always recognize problems as problems because things have always been that way. We are lulled into thinking that things are the way they are supposed to be. Changing your company's culture is hard but possible. The results are better for your employees and company if you stick with it.

Reflection

Are you collaborating now? Ask yourself this question and then look for evidence for your answer.

How are you selecting people for projects or initiatives? Do you look for the people and then ask them to complete a task, or do you identify the task and collect the people to complete the task? Depending on what you discover, you may need to revise the structures of your company. This approach requires flexibility rather than structures.

Where are your plans for projects or initiatives developed? Are they created at the source of the problem or are they created and/or challenged by people who will not implement the plans? How can you adjust your structure to be more flexible and hence accountable?

In the last part of the model, attention, which of the following are you doing well right now: accountability, problem identification, talents, and recognition?

▶ Why are you doing well in each area, or why not?

▶ Which areas can you work on to improve?

3

The Goal

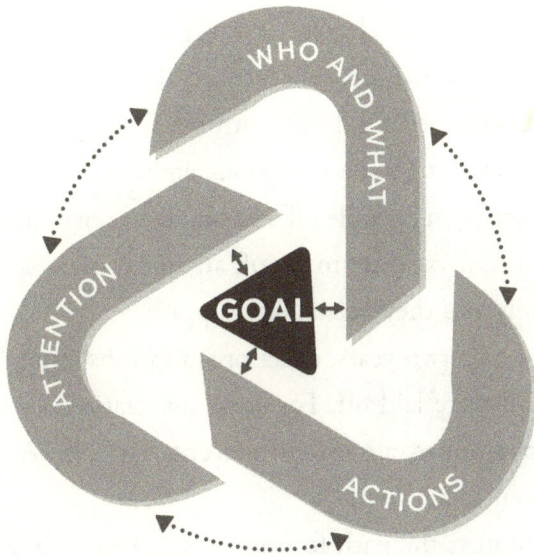

In the fall of 2008, I was beginning an exciting chapter in my leadership experience, when the great recession started. I became the Executive Director of what is now the National Science Teaching

Association (NSTA), an association that had about 350,000 members and a major capital campaign in progress. I knew this was going to be an exciting opportunity.

Something I had not considered when I accepted the position was that the economic indicators and forecasts were not looking good. No one knew how bad it was going to be or how long it would last. The members of NSTA are teachers and they do not have a lot of disposable income, so they could be affected more than some. My charge from the president of NSTA was to bring the association into the 21st century, and as I looked out over the horizon, it seemed more challenging than ever.

Initially I learned about NSTA by meeting with members and partners to ask what they valued and whether there were services we might provide. What I quickly realized, as the market crashed and investment banks were closing, was the economic downturn was going to be an external force that would affect all existing and new initiatives I had hoped for. I met with NSTA employees and it was obvious this was going to be an anxious time for them, as companies around us were laying people off and others weren't hiring. I made a commitment to myself not to lay off anyone if possible. NSTA was my new family and they needed my support.

Over the next two years, other organizations struggled as debts grew and staff were laid off. For some associations of similar size, membership dropped almost 30 percent. For NSTA, it dropped about 3 percent.

In this context the path forward was murky at best because of the fear of crashing along with many other businesses and associations. I remember telling the staff to look around at each other and remember we are the ones who have control of our destiny by the actions we take. We can't control the economy.

The leadership team revisited the NSTA goals several times early on, so we agreed on a goal that we were committed to. It was "to promote excellence and innovation in science teaching and learning for all." We had strategic sub-goals in several areas: advocacy, professional learning, standards, and membership. Our tactics to meet these sub-goals were to get closer to our members and customers by establishing stronger connections with committees and large state chapters, to focus on membership needs, and to examine what products and services we had that we could enhance. We had to make many quick decisions because the business world around us was not good. Our approach was to invest in connections and partnerships and use our few resources to try new things. The good news is we were able to accomplish many new things during this time of external crisis.

We made unique decisions to forge a path forward in the turmoil of the external environment. Our strategy was to connect with outside organizations to build new partnerships, products, and services, which allowed us to enhance and expand what we already did. One partnership included two large Washington, D.C., science-related institutions. This set up the association for future growth with potential for several new product lines when the economy turned around.

We invested in our people and potential instead of cutting back. We formed new collaborations with states, international sister associations, and cities where we hosted conferences. We created a new STEM-themed conference, an expanded digital product line, and a new CRM (customer relationship management) for members. We asked members what they wanted so we could better customize services and products. Finally, we were able to obtain the commitment of almost $34 million for the capital campaign. All of this focused work kept the association debt-free, and there were no layoffs.

The successes we accomplished were through focusing on our goals and through building relationships externally. This resulted in action by players who could see they would benefit by collaborating. By sticking to the plan, much was accomplished when many people viewed the situation as dire. It was not easy. Some people wanted to reduce the number of employees or conferences, or produce more of what we already offered. Collaboration and sticking to goals have positive results, but it can be difficult. Adjustments are often necessary while pursuing the larger goal.

Determining the Path

A goal on either a large or small scale helps employees and customers understand who you are and why you are in business. It is not really an elevator speech, but it should have the clarity of one. When the goal is clear, partners, suppliers, contractors, and providers know who you are and whether you are a competitor. This is why the goal is the most important part of the collaboration model.

When setting a goal, consider where you have been, what is happening externally with the general market, what is going on with your customers, and where you want to go in one, three, five, or 10 years. If you want to reach a new market share, you need to know what is happening in that ecosystem. Who are the customers and the competitors? How many potential products are there and what is their quality? How big is the customer potential?

The unknowns always make the process of setting a goal challenging. It's difficult to be clear in the murky world we live in now. At the same time, you can use what you now know to stretch into the future. The clarity is about the steps you should take to get there. While I am writing this, the world is experiencing a global pandemic. When will there be a vaccine? Will there be another pandemic?

These are questions few people have answers to or control over. In circumstances where the future is unclear, you can develop the goal based on what you *do* know. It is really all you have.

Spend time looking at the horizon—the past, present, and future—to build a common understanding of the factors that could affect the business. Outline what makes the greatest sense based on the current and future external context.

This can be done through a specific strategic planning process, such as Goal-Based Strategic Planning, SWOT (strengths, weaknesses, opportunities, and threats) or SWOC (strengths, weaknesses, opportunities, and challenges), gap planning, and balanced scorecard. Or you can use whatever data you have available to create a plan.

Identifying the factors that could affect the business and choosing the right goal to pursue is best done by involving others. This can be done with a few people or with hundreds. I once did this with hundreds. It was a bit chaotic, but using small groups, participants were able to express their reactions and knowledge. Sharing ideas and getting feedback is a critical step. Do others who have some knowledge of your business and intent believe these are the right goals? What things were missed because these people were not in the room when previous ideas were generated?

You are not trying to achieve consensus but rather are looking for levels of agreement. Experts and novices both can contribute much in this process. The group or team needs to know that not every idea will end up being used and that ultimately, a decision will be made by a small group. To narrow down the number of ideas, you can employ a prioritization process. Small teams suggest and combine their ideas, then a larger group narrows them down to the most important. Those lists can then be brought to another, larger group to prioritize. Repeat this to reduce the number of ideas down to three to eight. The team leading the effort should make the final priority decisions and they can also set up some small experiments to test them.

Testing Goal Ideas

The last step of testing goal ideas with others who know you is important. By sharing ideas and getting feedback, you are able to develop a broader understanding of the goals of your employees and partners.

When you determine a goal, you will not necessarily know it is the right goal. Alternative plans may be needed if the conditions change. Having a good feedback loop for the effectiveness of the goals you create and for outside factors will help you know when to make adjustments to the goal or stay the course.

Identify the context and narrow the direction of the goal, then regularly check it with others to encourage engagement. This builds confidence in the meaning of the goal.

Here is a simple exercise that will help you determine your goal:

I (We) want to accomplish _____ so we/customers can _____.

The first part of the statement is the goal, what you want to accomplish. The second part is the *purpose* of the goal, the reason behind it. The combination of these two things creates a common motivation that allows the team to work together.

Personal Goals

In addition to setting goals for your team or business, you probably also have personal goals. When assessing your path as an individual, reflect on what you really like to do. Many people don't do this and jump into positions or stay in positions too long. I realize that following your passion is not necessarily helpful guidance because your passion can change, depending on the culture or position within a particular company.

I enjoy seeing people engaged, learning, and growing. The reward in my work is seeing people engaged and happy with their results. This passion transcends the concept of a career path and provided me the flexibility to change jobs and stay true to what I really enjoy: being a teacher, nonprofit leader, leader of teams, organization chief executive, board chairperson, and coach or leader. I hope my choices have made the world a better place.

In your reflection, consider the context of the ecosystem we are in. Technology has made powerful tools and knowledge available to people all over the world, with big effects on how we work. These technologies facilitate the world's workers to compete with traditionally wealthy countries. Determining a work path can be limiting if it misses a larger purpose because companies and jobs are changing so fast that planning a career is almost impossible. It is not easy to see clearly, looking into the future, if a company or job will be around in 10 or 20 years. You must remain flexible in the new ecosystem.

Jobs have always changed, and with expanding trends in automation and artificial intelligence, many professional positions will be replaced. Therefore, developing a strategy for career *achievement* may be a better approach as career paths are no longer linear. Think about it as a scientist might: test out a job and decide if it is helping you achieve your goal. Every job is like running an experiment for your career.

A colleague asked me once, "What will be your legacy? What do you want to be remembered for when you are in your 80s or 90s or maybe older?" Hopefully I will get there. I am guessing people may not remember the job titles I once had. They will likely remember what impact I had on others and the difference I made in their lives.

Clayton Christensen, a major innovator, recently passed away. He believed his legacy would be measured at the individual level. He would ask his students in one of his graduate classes from Harvard to ask themselves three simple questions:

1. How can I be sure that I'll be happy in my career?

2. How can I be sure that my relationships with my spouse and my family become an enduring source of happiness?

3. How can I be sure I'll stay out of jail?

He explains this method in his classic article titled "How will you measure your life?" These are great questions to start thinking about your personal goals.

How does having a goal help you? There are plenty of people who have a job they thought they wanted. It gives them money and status, but they are frustrated, stressed, or exhausted because it doesn't meet their personal desire to do something meaningful. It is just a job. Many of those people will leave and look for another job. The sooner you do this the better, so you don't get trapped. Others will advise you to follow your passion. Simon Sinek, author, motivational speaker, and organizational consultant, is known for recommending you know your "why." Is what you are doing right now helping you accomplish your "why," or your purpose? What do you want most for your business, your family, and yourself? How do these desires align with the work you do and the decisions you are making for your company?

Asking yourself these questions is the first step to gaining clarity. When you have clarity about what you are working toward, you are able to prioritize and align your life and business practices to values that are effective in achieving your goal.

The key to achieving your goal is looking wider. If your current position is not satisfying your sense of success, setting the goal to get a promotion is not looking wider. Let's say you are a leader of a team. The team doesn't seem to be interacting well or reaching their KPIs. Maybe there is not much trust among team members. You begin to question your role and whether you are the right person for the job. Instead of pushing harder on accountability measures, stop and ask why you accepted the role in the first place. What about the company do you like?

Let's say you determine you want to stay and you are excited about initiating changes to make a greater difference through the company. You want to lead others to be successful. What do you need to do to lead others to success? Do they know how their roles fit into the larger company success? These are wider questions that affect motivation. If you can have a highly functioning team that meets deadlines and has fun at the same time, the company is accomplishing its goal.

Maybe you want to learn a new skill or want to know how another industry works. Then your goal is to learn and expand your knowledge and skills. Go back to school or participate in activities where you learn with others, such as mastermind groups or online courses. To engage others, it is helpful if the goal is something they can participate in too. Making a distinction between personal and organizational goals is important for motivating others.

Understanding what motivates you will help you navigate opportunities as they are presented to you. When choosing a path, I advocate for thinking and reacting.

▶ Develop a goal that is intrinsic, one that is transferrable to other positions, jobs, companies, and fields. This goal should be something that motivates you.

▶ Develop a strategy for types of positions to help feed your motivation and contribute to your goal.

▶ Experience various types of work to learn what motivates you and how your current position drives or hinders that.

▶ Learn to both narrow and broaden your knowledge with the intent of helping you become flexible and an expert.

Which steps have you already done? What do you want to do next? Ask yourself the following questions:

▶ What am I doing now that makes me feel I am making a difference?

▶ What do I want to do to add value for myself and/or for my company?

▶ What strengths do I have or could I build that, if used more often or differently, could make a greater impact?

▶ What knowledge or skills do I not have that could help me make a greater impact?

▶ What does the impact of doing these things look like?

Organizational Goals and Purpose

From a leadership position within an organization, how can you align your goals and the organization's goals? What do you want to accomplish that will extend beyond your time at that organization? This is very important. It is what your legacy at that company will be.

Competition is a potential barrier to understanding collaboration. It is assumed that if you are collaborating you don't compete. This isn't correct. You may collaborate to meet a goal, but in other areas compete. One team might collaborate with another team on solving a logistic or software problem, but they compete on the quality of handling customers. Similarly, competing businesses may collaborate to make improvements to their shared industry or to the world in general.

Some shifts are occurring in business mindsets in regard to goals and competition, but it will take a long time before most businesses have broad goals that impact the greater good of the ecosystem and the world.

One indicator of change in the direction of being more purposeful comes from the Business Roundtable, an influential group of business leaders. Here is how they describe themselves: "Business Roundtable members are the chief executive officers of leading U.S. companies. Collectively, they represent every sector of the economy and bring a unique and important perspective to bear on policy issues that impact the economy. Roundtable members are thought leaders, advocating for policy solutions that foster U.S. economic growth and competitiveness."

About 200 members issued a statement that said, "While each of our individual companies serves its own corporate purpose, we share a fundamental commitment to all our stakeholders." This statement made headlines and became the topic of editorials and questions about whether they really meant it. The intent as I understand it is to move to being more purpose driven and less driven by profit.

Deloitte, in partnership with Forbes Insights (2020), recently found two-thirds of global business leaders say their budgets for programs with purpose have increased from previous years. A study by Welch and Yoon (2020) found that ESG (environmental, social, and governance) investments created no difference in the performance of companies overall, however, employee satisfaction was much greater. I would like you to look for a pattern in how these companies have broadened their purpose (goals). These companies have been working as good corporate citizens for some time, so this is not completely out of character for a business.

- PepsiCo's Indra Nooyi championed "Performance with Purpose" for over 15 years, meeting ambitious internal yardsticks on nutrition such as eliminating trans-fats, reducing sugar and sodium, and environmental sustainability milestones on recyclable packaging and responsible water use.

- Years ago, Paul Polman of Unilever launched its "Sustainable Living Plan," which set ambitious goals such as cutting Unilever's environmental impact in half by 2030.

- Merck's Ken Frazier told me, "Businesses exist to deliver value to society." Merck has existed for 126 years.

- Ed Stack, the CEO of Dick's Sporting Goods, didn't await a shareholder vote before pledging to stop selling assault-style weapons and high-capacity magazines and to require age limits for gun purchases and call for universal background checks.

- ▶ Ginni Rometty of IBM has modeled responsible stewardship of data as a core principle with transparency and ownership of data, as well as massive investment in technology education, to "new collar" workers who could have been left behind without higher educational credentials.

- ▶ Walmart, the nation's largest employer, has raised wages, triggering parallel moves by other major retailers. Walmart is also providing training to hundreds of thousands of its associates through its Academies program and initiatives to allow associates to pursue college degrees debt-free, for $1 per day.

- ▶ Walgreens created "Balance Rewards for healthy choices," a healthcare innovation in the form of a retail loyalty program.

- ▶ Goldman Sachs' 10,000 Women initiative has been investing in female entrepreneurs to foster economic growth and stronger communities in 56 countries.

- ▶ JP Morgan's Jamie Dimon announced its $500 million Advancing Cities initiative, driving inclusive growth and creating greater economic opportunities in cities across the world, building a proven model for impact in Detroit, Chicago, and Washington, D.C., by combining the firm's lending capital, philanthropic capital, and expertise to make investments in cities.

These companies are incorporating purpose into business plans. This focus can have many benefits for employees and customers. It also requires some different thinking and actions. They need partners or organizations that can help them identify and implement many of these efforts. Collaboration has become a requirement to meet the purposes they have identified.

Wanting to be successful or the best in the industry is not the type of goal that motivates others. Wanting to help people live better lives, solve a health crisis, or help people out of tragic legal situations are goals that motivate. The second most common reason for employees to say they are not engaged (right after having a bad boss) is not feeling that what they are doing is contributing to anything. Striving for greater goals and sharing them with the team will better engage them. Byron Clayton shared in a 2015 *Frontiers in Psychology* article that a shared vision is the highest predictor of a successful merger and acquisition.

Putting some parameters around the goal is also helpful. What is the measure of success? Who should be involved? How long will we work on this? Then everyone knows what the level of commitment is and the scope of the initiative.

The heart of collaborative leadership is selecting motivating goals and creating a shared vision with the team.

Defining your goal is the first step to developing a strategy for handling the complexity of the world today. An important aspect of this is to ask, "What would the impact be if we succeeded?"

This question will help drive everyone. If you can visualize how you, the company, the country, or world will be different, that becomes the motivation of the team. This is important on a personal level but critical at the cross-department and company level. The participants will need to be continually reminded of where you are heading because the work may be hard and giving up is the easy solution.

Defining your path forward is done through reflection, analysis, discussion, and commitment. Always give yourself time to focus on the horizon or broader goal to remember what you are aiming for.

Getting Team Members On Board

There are several ways you can increase the engagement and performance of employees. Purpose is one of those factors. Having a clear and meaningful goal is like knowing the ending of a movie before you plan on seeing it. You know how the story is going to end but you don't necessarily know how you will get there. Think of how popular the movie *Titanic* was when it came out. Everyone knew the ending and they still flocked to see it. Your team has to know where you are headed and be willing to tackle the challenges that will arise during the journey. If they think the goal is too big, unrealistic, or too easy, they will not work hard for you.

Your team needs to make a commitment to the goal. They will experience hard work, perhaps long hours, and possibly some hardship along the way. They need to understand the role they will play in getting to that goal. To help them make that commitment, you can involve them in the creation of the goal by doing several things:

1. Collect their feedback on the draft goals.

2. Participate in the goal-setting process.

3. Identify faults in the goal(s) so adjustments can be made.

4. Articulate the processes needed to start achieving the goal and make sure they have the leadership support or authority to do those things.

5. Collect feedback along every step of development of the goals.

6. Ensure they are recognized for their contribution.

This story may or may not be true, but it is an excellent example of how you help a team know the expectation before they start. Ernest Shackleton, who led three expeditions to the Antarctic, posted an advertisement for his crew. It said, "Men wanted for hazardous journey, small wages, bitter cold, long months of complete darkness, constant danger, safe return doubtful, and honor and recognition in event of success."

The ad was clear and listed expectations and possible outcomes but not how each day was going to play out. It did not outline performance expectations or the actions they would be taking but rather set the parameters by which all other activities would fit. Too lofty goals often seem disingenuous, so be careful in how the goal is crafted. You want your team to be as willing to go the distance with you as Shackleton's did, so work for clarity and openness.

Reflection

As a summary of this chapter, the goal is the larger purpose and develops or creates shared interest.

Convene your team and ask the following questions:

- ▶ How do we want to add value to the impact of our company?

- ▶ What strengths do we have that if we used them differently could make a great impact?

- ▶ What other people could join our team, either in the short term or longer term, for us to have a greater impact?

- ▶ What would the impact be if we succeeded?

Convene a group of people from related departments within the company or companies and ask these questions:

- ▶ What could we do to add value to each of our groups/companies that would benefit all of us?

- ▶ What strengths do we have that if we used them differently and together could make a great impact for both of us?

- ▶ What other people/companies could join our group, either in the short term or longer term, for us to have a greater impact?

- ▶ What would the impact be if we succeeded?

4

Convene the Team

"Engineering serendipity is this idea that we can help people come across unexpected but helpful connections better than at a random rate. And in some ways, it's based on trying to reassess this notion of serendipitous as lucky— to think of serendipitous as smart."

—Ethan Zuckerman
(American media scholar, blogger, and internet activist)

Backstage Capital (BackstageCapital.com) is a venture capital firm that began with a very defined focus for their investments. Their strategy and reason for existence was and still is to foster inclusivity. This may seem odd for a VC firm, as traditional VCs by nature are exclusive in who they select and invest in. They work through existing networks such as connected universities, referrals, or endorsements from people they already know. This makes sense for traditional VCs in terms of having the greatest confidence in where they will invest funds and get a return. They live in an ecosystem that makes sense for them, but minority communities or minority entrepreneurs are essentially left out of the typical VC firm ecosystem.

What do I mean? Most minorities do not have a history or legacy of attending elite universities to build a network or get referrals. They are not able to connect easily or know someone who could give them a referral. This is not always the case, but generally it is true. If you receive an investment, you are more likely to get another, so a smaller and smaller pool of people get a large portion of the investments.

On their website, Backstage Capital says, "Backstage Capital invests in startup founders who identify as a Woman, Person of Color, and/or LGBTQ. We believe these founders are underestimated and have the most potential for unlocking innovation and creating valuable businesses." This pool of people currently lives in a different VC ecosystem than the traditional one I described above.

This statement on the Backstage Capital website is clear and their purpose is well laid out. There is little to question about who they are and what they do.

Backstage Capital has an open application process for funding requests and if someone has a good idea, they do not need an introduction or network referral. Backstage Capital tries to streamline the investment process so the wait time is not as long as other VCs. They create systems to help people become successful. They work with their investments by connecting them to other resources, such as a big VC group or another company, so their client can advance from the original investment. They are in a sense creating a new ecosystem.

What intrigued me about Backstage Capital was how they are focused on their purpose. They have found a way to utilize a broad array of people and organizations within and outside the VC ecosystem to accomplish their purpose. Their purpose is value driven, need based, and very important for innovation and economic diversity, while not being blinded by the trappings of focusing on only developing companies for financial gain.

Their purpose draws people who have a similar purpose. Being clear about your organizational purpose is critical today, with a workforce that is mobile and looking for purpose. Recruiting and retaining employees is challenging but much easier when the purpose is clear.

Finding the right people to participate with you is about more than just finding the best workers—the A players. If your purpose is strong enough it will be an attractor. Descriptions of successful companies include being attractor companies. Employees want to work there. They want to participate in their work, not just have a job. When people want to be at a particular company, they are excited and want to learn.

Dr Lloyd S. Nelson, teacher of statistics and prolific author, was referred to in W. Edwards Deming's *Out of the Crisis* for his observation: "The most important figures that one needs for management are unknown or unknowable, but successful management must nevertheless take them into account."

The quote Dr. Nelson is most often known for is "Failure to understand variation is a central problem of management." We know from many studies that diversity in the workforce and on teams gives us variation and there are great benefits to it. However, diversity is not a focus for many companies, as they want people to tie into company culture.

When working with people, teams, partners, and collaborators, participants are unlikely to agree on many things. To apply the model for collaboration, you must be open-minded, make mistakes, support others, and be willing to give up some control. That is learning in real time.

Select the Players

How do you know who to choose to work on a collaborative effort? HR professionals in some companies have systems for hiring, but it's less common to have systems for choosing individuals for specific projects or initiatives.

When assembling a team for a collaborative project or potential collaborative merger, ask yourself some questions:

- ▶ Who do you work with whom you respect and trust?

- ▶ Who in other companies do you respect and trust?

- ▶ Who is able to make critical decisions at the right level for this project?

- ▶ Who is able to engage others in helping to solve a problem?

- ▶ Who is confident enough in their own abilities to listen to others?

- ▶ Who is effective in carrying out an initiative?

▶ Who is creative?

▶ Who knows the market and who is able to add value to make this project greater?

These questions are more about insights, character, and behavior rather than knowledge of logistics. People who are effective at building a collaborative environment do not limit their view of the potential in people to their past skills but look to see how they can grow. They have an open mindset about people. Good players can be flexible in their thinking and adjust as needed, while maintaining discipline and performance.

Three Leadership Styles

Leaders are found at every level of a company. They are not limited by their position within the company. Finding these people and observing their skills in working with others is a great beginning for selecting the right people. Three types of leadership help identify which people are needed to work together for a particular project or initiative.

Ron Price and Stacy Ennis discuss leadership styles in more depth in *Growing Influence* (2018). The three types are Positional, Expert, and Character leadership.

The *Positional leader* is the leader with a title. It is temporary because when the person leaves, the title changes. They can make decisions and influence the process, but only as long as they have that position. This role is often more directive. It can also function in connected leadership by taking a role for a set amount of time.

Expert leaders are the people who know a lot about a topic, discipline, or project and bring their expert knowledge to the table. This role is often more advisory.

Character leadership supersedes details. You trust these leaders because they do what they say. If committed to a project, they are willing to make compromises, influence others, and lead through their integrity or character. You can count on these people over time. This role is more collaborative and connected to others.

Have you seen these three types of leaders in your company?

Which of the three types of leaders should lead a collaborative project? There is no right answer, as some individuals can be more than one type of leader. So much depends on context, the level of development the initiative is in, and what needs to be accomplished. Has the project been going on for a while and needs a boost or a reassessment, or is it new and in need of organizing?

For the broadest oversight, the Character leader will have many advantages. The very nature of a collaborative project means it will likely have networked leaders throughout, who may take the reins for a short time and then give them back. It takes a special kind of person to be comfortable enough in their abilities to facilitate this type of shared or connected leadership.

The different leadership styles could be the same person playing a different role. Expert leaders are needed for knowledge and skills in many aspects of a project. And of course, a Positional leader will be necessary either for policy decisions or clearing barriers. Hence, they do not have to be a part of every decision, just those that might slow or prevent forward movement.

Beyond the leadership skills of individuals, consider what they can bring to a discussion depending on how they think. Bringing together the right diverse group of people with the right skills is becoming easier than it was in the past. By identifying a task in the goal-setting process, you'll be able to identify who will be the best to carry it out.

A team of engineers carrying out a merger plan with many subtle people interactions and relationship building may not be the best choice because they may be more motivated by getting the job done and less by the relationship building. Conversely a design project between two companies may not need people skills but more creative and technical skills. Having a homogeneously structured team can derail a project before it even gets going.

There are a number of psychological assessment tools that help identify people's behavioral and skill strengths. These tools can guide you to better identify the behaviors of individuals on a team and look for gaps, then fill those gaps by adding people with strengths that will advance the project faster.

Evans Baiya and *The Innovator's Advantage* program (TheInnovatorsAdvantage.com) have developed a system that takes this to another level. The result is an innovation fitness report that identifies the skills of an individual for particular aspects of the innovation cycle. For example, some people are better at ideation and others at testing or scaling. The leader in particular parts of an innovation cycle requires different strengths to be most effective.

It is important to not let others do all the work. There is a need at times for a singular decision-maker. Know when to step up and when to step back. Connected leadership is shared and can even be external to the team or organization. This allows for innovation, creativity, and developing and implementing exciting things because of the new interactions and diversity.

Utilizing players' strengths in this way encourages new combinations of people with different skills as the project progresses.

Keeping the same people on a team throughout the process may slow it or even derail it, as the team may not have the strengths to see through the challenges that arrive. A common error is to keep the same people together for too long. Some companies repeatedly move people around on teams to experience new things, learn, and add their unique skills to other teams.

Define Roles

Employees are most effective and happiest when they are using their strengths. Employees are most productive when they enjoy their work. It follows then to design jobs or roles based on their strengths. This is not commonly done, and it requires a different type of thinking in the selection of teams based on expertise and capabilities rather than titles and positions. The traditional system of seniority or hierarchies makes this strategy more difficult.

An easier shift to make is to involve employees in the goal and plan development. They have a better sense of logistical concerns, which allows those concerns to be raised earlier rather than later. They may also have had more time to think about what needs to happen, so when you are ready to deploy the plan, they have already considered how to do it.

Designing positions based on strengths and involving employees in the goal and plan development will add to the strength, quality, and resulting performance of the initiative.

While roles may change throughout a collaboration, there are roles that can be identified prior to starting because they are common. These roles may be always, sometimes, or occasionally active. At the same time there are some roles that will surface while in the middle or end of the project.

1. Active Roles

Some roles that are active throughout the entire project include an oversight leader and experts in the discipline area. These roles may not be active all the time as the oversight leader needs to check in and learn where the effort is going so they can help with policy or barriers that might arise. This person needs skills in project management, self-management, teamwork, and interpersonal skills.

2. Dormant Roles

Some roles are periodic. These roles are for people who might collect data, share expertise in a particular area, or design. These are the experts. They might have an intense period of work and then never be needed again. Or they might come in and out of the picture based on their expertise. Their skills are specialized and used to enhance or inform decisions.

3. Monitoring Roles

Monitoring roles could be seen as active, but they are only in the picture periodically. The leadership fills this role as the initiative will likely need their direct support occasionally. HR would play a role here, either assisting with selecting people or in monitoring the impact of the group from a people perspective. Project analysts or evaluators would have a similar role but would look at business performance and milestone achievement.

4. Partnership Roles

Lastly there are partnership roles. These people need skills of communication, persuasion, and connection. They are often the glue to ensure relationships are built and maintained. The people involved have to feel connected even if they are not working with others on a regular basis. The people in partnership roles are known by top leadership and can go to them if a problem arises.

Define Activities

To plan and launch a successful collaboration, expertise is needed for different phases. The larger the collaboration, the more differentiation of roles is needed. For example, the early design and planning phases require different expertise than metric development and measurement phases. Some roles require political skill while others require analytical skills. Here is a list of some types of expertise.

Designing: This type of activity includes ideating, prioritizing, involving feedback, and researching and organizing information in some way that is useful to others.

Planning: This type of activity is similar to traditional project management skills. It includes determining what comes first, what capacities are needed, both human and material/equipment, and outlining when something must start so that the next activity can take place when it is needed.

Coordinating: This type of activity is people intensive. The role requires strong interpersonal skills, diplomacy and tact, persuasion, communication, conflict negotiation, and connection. The people involved in a collaboration are highly skilled in very different areas so the activity requires a person to successfully move among these people to keep things on track with as little disruption as possible.

Supporting: This type of activity is often thought of as administrative, but this work is also a type of coordination. They connect among others and sometimes across levels within an organization. These positions often respond well to others who care about what they do.

Overseeing: This type of activity extends the leadership role throughout the collaboration. This way, decisions can be made quickly without having to wait for others to decide. From the top-level CEO or team leader, an awareness of the roles and respect for the knowledge of people who know about the work is helpful. They can also clear the way for policy or have access to necessary budgets and materials.

Testing: This type of work is often analytical but also can be very social. Testing describes the shorter-term test of an idea, not the longer-term evaluation work. It is a social activity, testing new behaviors that team members are working on. It's also analytical in that it may require looking at the numbers of social tests or engineering of a product.

Evaluating: This type of activity is generally more analytical and summative. It can also be short term, such as with performance reviews. This activity examines the performance of a product or message to determine its effectiveness.

Deploying: This type of activity is a combination of the traditional sales and program follow-through. Many efforts fail because of their inability to deploy effectively.

These actions are not mutually exclusive and can overlap. Think hard about who is doing what part of the work at what time in the process.

There is another type of expertise for the leader. I am going to call it the Multiplier. This is a term used by Liz Wiseman in her book *Multipliers.*

Multiplier: This type of activity is a kind of jet fuel for developing others. Leaders can amplify the expertise and capabilities of the employees around them and in their organization. They can inspire others to stretch themselves to deliver results when it may not even be their job.

Thinking about the role of leadership is critical in a collaboration. If the same leader on a team does all of these roles, they will likely miss many aspects that someone with a strength in that area would add. These actions are areas people play within. See the chart below for some examples. Being flexible, continuing to learn, and being creative are skills of the future.

Roles in Parts of the Model

Role	The Goal	Who and What	Actions	Attention
Designing	X	X		X
Planning	X	X	X	X
Coordinating		X	X	X
Supporting		X	X	X
Overseeing	X	X	X	
Testing			X	X
Evaluating			X	X
Deploying		X	X	
Multiplier		X	X	

Assign Roles

The key to active roles, dormant roles, monitoring roles, and partnership roles working well together is a shared purpose. You will bring the players together periodically for review, updates on progress, and problem-solving adjustments. So how do you choose the people to fit these roles? The best method is to pick people who agree on the purpose but may not agree on how to get there. This will give you the widest set of options to consider, though it may also cause conflict.

By choosing individuals with different ideas and opinions, you design "collisions" into the interactions of the group. I use the term collisions here to indicate something different than normal group interaction. Brené Brown in *Dare to Lead* uses the term "rumble." She includes setting boundaries and clear expectations as a part of the "rumble." The word implies more than being polite and going with the group.

For example, a leadership team or group of managers from different departments, divisions, or from outside are mixed together to help solve a problem. The collection of people facilitates bumping into other people's beliefs, knowledge, and perspectives. A group where the members come from different perspectives can conceive of solutions that address the whole problem collectively. Unique things happen in groups like this. One way to keep a lid on conflict is to continue to remind everyone of the purpose and clarify boundaries and expectations. Don't allow people to get personal or go off topic.

Jack McGuinness wrote in his article "Great Leadership Teams Optimize Collaboration" about the important features of effective teams and how they optimize effective collaboration. It's important to gain clarity on the purpose and how to integrate it with the way people work on the team. The foundational work of gaining clarity on the purpose can seem slow, but without a strong purpose, floundering and miscues are more frequent. Integrate the purpose in how the team works by reinforcing collaboration principles. McGuinness also lists skills for effective collaboration and, while they may not be new, they are hard to do.

Here is his list:

- ▶ **Communication**. Be clear, direct, and honest, and speak often.

- ▶ **Listening**. Encourage respect by communicating "I value you."

▶ **Feedback**. Give and receive feedback and adjust accordingly.

▶ **Compromise**. Seek to understand and then compromise. Being a humble leader promotes this.

▶ **Dependability**. Be accountable to yourself and your team.

This list can be helpful anytime but particularly when a new team is formed or a team needs to improve their teamwork. Working on these skills will improve communication, reduce workplace conflict, identify the emotional impact of discussions, and uncover hidden skills.

When assigning roles, you will need to choose individuals to fill those roles. The "Convene the Team" or "Who" aspect of the model does not define the specific people who should be involved in a collaborative effort, but rather the characteristics and capabilities required. It addresses the type of people needed and the leader's role.

If you haven't already, do a self-assessment of your behaviors, motivation, and skills. This is different from a personality assessment. One that I like to use is TTI Success Insights' TriMetrixHD, which is a great catalyst for conversation about strengths of individuals in the team and what is missing. You can also ask your team members what their strengths are. As a leader, spend some time examining your team's strengths. Ask yourself, "Which of these can be used to leverage the best from my team members, and what do I add to the team that is of real value? How can I mitigate or look for someone to help fill in those areas of weakness?"

When assigning roles, you also must pay attention to behaviors others are exhibiting. Make observation a kind of anthropologic task where you record patterns of behaviors and the way people on the team talk.

▶ Do they listen?

▶ How much do they talk?

▶ When they talk, do people seem to listen?

▶ Do they support others?

▶ Do they take the lead sometimes and give it away other times?

▶ Do they volunteer for things?

▶ Do they define the purpose of the discussion?

This is by no means a comprehensive list of questions, but it's a good place to start to identify people who may be appropriate fits for the roles you need.

From your observations, make a list of people who can be flexible, supportive, focused, and goal-oriented to join the collaborative effort. If you are assembling a team for a merger or an alliance, it will require a different level of focus than an internal project because the scope is very different.

You might use a scenario planning template to help with this process. Here is an example:

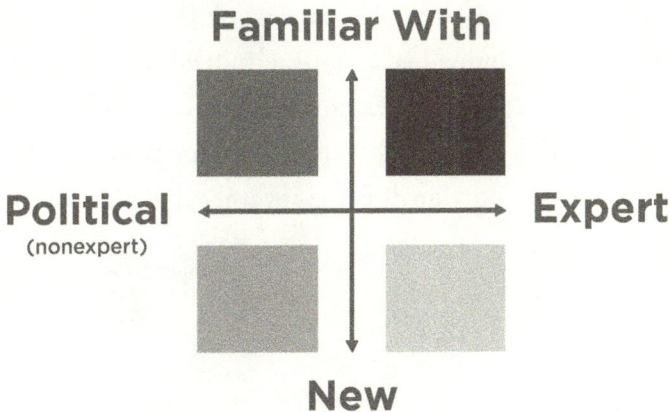

Familiar With

Political (nonexpert) ← → **Expert**

New

This model allows you to compare people you know versus those you don't and experts versus nonexperts who are politically adept. For a more technical task, you may want someone who is both an expert and familiar or someone who is new to you and an expert. For a task that requires persuasion, you might want someone who is politically adept rather than an expert.

Once you have assembled the team, you will need to pay attention to make adjustments and move people on and off the team as the effort develops. Having new people at different stages of a project or for different functions is the best way to take advantage of the new ideas and energy brought on by those changes. Regularly revisit the purpose of the team and their behaviors, then either continue to develop them for working together or bring new people into the team.

Team Versus Individual Incentives

Most CEOs understand that effective teams are critical. The challenge they have is identifying the right combination of players within their organization who are capable of developing winning products and taking them to market. Because of this, many of the incentive systems in the workplace are not aligned to teams but to individuals, and the individual is the wrong unit of analysis. It's more important to incentivize the team because especially in larger organizations, innovation happens when groups of individuals come together to design and support an initiative.

Reflection

Getting the right people in the collaboration is critical. They should have the right skills and be in the right places to do the best work. You must support them at every stage.

1. When you have the option of drawing people in from other parts of the company or locations, here are some questions you can ask:

    ▶ What is it you want to accomplish (the goal)?

    ▶ Are you really clear about the purpose?

    ▶ Do you know your value? What about the value of others?

    ▶ What are the strengths necessary for this team?

    ▶ What role(s) will each member play, including you?

    ▶ How big is this effort? How many other collaborators are involved? What roles do they have?

    ▶ What investment, both in time and financially, can you make to support this team?

    ▶ How long will the team be together?

    ▶ How will you measure whether the team has been effective?

2. Another approach to finding the right people is to use a scenario planning template. You have your existing team or people you are familiar with—place them in the sectors in this tool to see how balanced your team will be:

Familiar With

Political (nonexpert) ⟷ **Expert**

New

3. If you are in a smaller organization or team and are unable to draw from other places for team members, approach this part of the collaboration model with an open mindset. What skills do you need to build on the team?

▶ The questions above can help in that process. Start by answering them. List the skills available to you.

▶ What are the blind spots that might exist when your team is working together?

▶ Once you've identified the skills and blind spots, record them and post them for the team to see. This will help them understand what could divert them. These need to be written positively, as this is not meant to be a list of criticisms.

▶ If a skill or blind spot is improved, then take it off the list. If a skill or blind spot is identified, add it to the list.

5

Carry Out the Plan

"Learn how to see. Realize that everything connects to everything else."

—Leonardo da Vinci

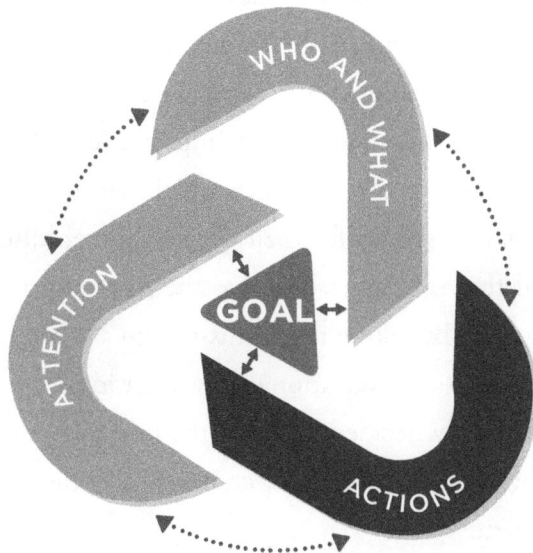

A team in a small company was struggling to agree on how to handle a project that needed to merge two public-facing healthcare database systems. One of the data systems was new and had to be designed and the other one was older and had not had an update in functionality for years. The members of the team agreed that the design of the new system had features that made it easier for the user to access the data. The older system was familiar and was not broken, and the user feedback was generally positive—so why change it?

Most of the team wanted to improve the older system and design a new and improved system that would integrate the two systems together. To do this, they would need to reorganize the older system's data. The part of the team that wanted to leave the older system as is voiced their disagreement, which stalled action and resulted in delaying the project. The majority of the team wanted to move forward with the design of the new system and the older one so they could be merged. Unfortunately, the redesign couldn't go forward until there was a decision about what to do with the older system.

The team leader wanted the team members to agree on what would happen. The leader's goal was to have everyone on the team see the new combined system as an improvement. The leader decided to revisit the goal of the project, which was to develop the best health information system for their users. Through discussion, the team realized that this larger goal was the right one and that they must act together. By taking the discussion up a conceptual level to the goal, it opened a conversation about other ideas.

The team finally decided it was in the best interest of the users to move forward. They had trust, confidence in each other, and a plan to complete.

By revisiting the goal, the team members remembered *why* they were working together and got out of the details of *how*. Having a clear goal helps most people act in the service of the goal rather than their personal agendas.

The leader had several choices. They could have said, "We are going to have two separate systems and let the users figure it out." They could have told the team members they had to modify their database whether they wanted to or not. They could have gone behind the scenes and met with the individuals who didn't want to change and tried to convince them. However the choice they made was the best one in terms of sustainability of the team because the team members reaffirmed why they were working on this project.

Employees are more motivated when they work for a purpose greater than themselves. In this case, the purpose of their work was for their users.

Determine the Actions

When organizing a collaboration, go slow at first to go fast. When the first parts of the model are in place (the goal and the players), the plan to action is fairly straightforward. Begin with the end in mind. Start with the clear and motivating purpose or goal you defined in chapter 3:

I (We) want to accomplish _____ so we/customers can

_____.

How will you know if you're on the path to accomplishing your goal? Most things can be measured today through metrics and tools. You can look at early, immediate, and long-term metrics. For example, say you want to have the highest quality product. To learn whether you are getting there, an early metric might be whether the product has low defects in the production process. An intermediate metric might be how well the product performs in field tests and with early customers. A long-term metric might be the percentage of return customers and positive feedback on social media.

Setting up clear measurements is the next step. We should measure what we think is important. Fill in the blanks:

I (We) will measure _____ and _____ at _____ points in time over the production and use of the product.

Consider how you will decide what to do if you run into problems. If you have people from different teams, divisions, or companies, this step is very important. Once the decision-making process is established, when you do run into a challenge, a decision can be made quickly. No part of the system should dispute the decision because they did not have a say in it.

If my metrics for the milestone selected are within the range _____ to _____, the next steps will be _____, and _____ team/person will make the decision about how to proceed.

Now you are ready to write a plan of action.

Write the Plan of Action

All the work up to this point sets the stage so when things happen, corrections and adaptations can occur.

Who will act in these roles? _____

This project/task _____ will start _____ and end _____. (You may need several of these statements for different parts of the project.)

Where will things occur? _____

If you have a progress monitor, then a reviewer, _____, will report on progress at _____ points in time.

If you prefer, you can use a project management tool instead of these questions.

The Parts of a Collaborative Project

A complex project or initiative has many dimensions to it and stages as it progresses. One way to think about a collaboration is through the outcome and likely participants. Collaborations can take many forms, from two people to multiple organizations with thousands of people. The chart below may help clarify some of the many different types of collaborations.

Collaboration Example for the Business Ecosystem

Who	Example	Outcome	Example
2 People	Project	Individual and/or project success	Two people work together to produce a new marketing logo.
3-12 People	Team Project	Team success	Members use their specific expertise to develop a strategy report for their department.
2 Departments	Intra-Organizational Project	Department and company success	Engineering and manufacturing departments engage to complete a total redesign and retooling of a manufacturing process.
Department and External Partner/Alliance	Inter-Organizational Project	Organization and partner project success	A department engages outside partners to complete the production and delivery of a new financial management software application to bring to market.
Departments and Internal and/or External Partners	Organizational Operation	Organization and partner success	The organization has multiple departments and partners, such as suppliers, transportation, subcontractors, and HR, which work together to accomplish a successful merger or acquisition.

You've already determined the types of actions that need to be taken when you assigned roles during the "Convene the Team" step of the model. Many of these actions overlap, and the larger the project, the more differentiation there will be between roles. You'll create a plan using these actions:

▶ Designing

▶ Planning

▶ Coordinating

▶ Supporting

▶ Overseeing

▶ Testing

▶ Evaluating

▶ Deploying

▶ Multiplier

Start with the design and planning steps for the collaboration, and your plan should outline the actions that are needed after that. The team who is carrying out the actions at that point knows what needs to happen next. They might be able to pass their work on to the next team as was outlined. Or if something changed, then they could decide where the work should go or check in with the leading team and have them decide.

The leading team should include some members who are doing the work and some members who are focused on management and policy, including the oversight leader. Remember, a group of people is not the same as a team. Many groups are not nearly as effective as they could be. Teamwork requires a challenging purpose and guidance around roles, timelines, and milestone. If there is a lead team, they should be allowed to intervene, end, or support a direction the work is going based on feedback they get during the collaboration.

Finding the right people to lead and to take the necessary actions is a combination of art and science. The art aspect is using behaviors you observe in employees you know and/or based on the recommendations of others. The science is to use behavioral and other assessments. For example, do you need an analyzer or idea generator?

With a complex project or merger, it would be a good idea to develop a job description based on what you want to happen. Then look at candidates and assess them to determine if their strength is needed for that position. *The Innovator's Advantage* by Evans Baiya and Ron Price described six Innovation Fitness Blueprints that included the ideal combination of talent, skills, and passion needed in an individual to excel at each of the six stages of innovation (Identify, Define, Develop, Verify, Deploy, and Scale). While each person is a unique combination of talent, skills, and passion, knowing what needs to be a person's strong suit for each project type will enhance your odds for success.

I am a great believer in psychology as a valuable tool for finding the right people. Without it, you can fall into internal biases such as cultural fits, similar thinkers, racial or ethnic similarities, and recommendations that the candidate is a friend or a good person. By including an impersonal component in the selection process, you reduce these biases. This is key in identifying people who think differently.

There is a saying that we hire for skills and fire for behavior. This stems from the idea that by just looking at someone on paper or having an interview with them, we miss a lot about them. With a behavioral assessment such as DISC, you can identify tendencies in normal and high-pressure situations as well as best ways to communicate with an individual. There are 12 dimensions to the TTI Success Insights motivation assessment, which helps you understand the motivations of people. I also suggest leadership competencies assessments. Each of these tools can reveal aspects of a person and should only be used to help with particular positions.

Adapting the Plan

When you're creating the plan to reach your goal, build in metrics and indicators that tell you what to pay attention to. Monitoring these will help you know when things begin to go off course or don't meet expectations earlier rather than at the end of a cycle or project. I call this aspect of the model "Attention" because it is all about paying attention. I will go into more detail about this in the next chapter. Remember, the model is not linear—you will need to pay attention throughout and may return to the planning phase to make adjustments as necessary. It is critical to be looking, measuring, and adjusting throughout the process.

You should set up weekly meetings with each team member and have collaborative update meetings with all the partners involved. Communication is most important to catching problems or mistakes and identifying problems before they grow too big.

A CEO who asks his team members to bring him problems, not solutions, is one who is curious and wants to explore many ideas for solutions. This is contrary to what you hear most of the time—it is essentially a cultural change. This facilitates having many people thinking through the solution rather than one person. As a result, the team members are more invested in the solution and they have the power of more ideas in tackling the problem.

Communication also keeps everyone updated on progress so you know when to recognize, acknowledge, and celebrate milestones.

Reflection

Once a collaboration begins, several features and factors need to be tended. Much of it relates to getting along, finding solutions, and building new relationships. This is the part of a collaboration that many people jump into without doing the harder goal-setting, planning, and people work first.

1. Complete the exercise from the chapter. Set up clear measurements for the task and timeline.

    I (We) will measure _____ and _____ at _____ points in time over the production and use of the product.

2. What should you do if you run into problems? Particularly if you have people from different teams, divisions, or companies, thinking through this step is very important. Determine a process for the various scenarios. List some possibilities. (Remember blame is not one of them.)

    If my metrics for the milestone selected are within the range _____ to _____, the next steps will be _____, and _____ team/person will make the decision about how to proceed.

3. Establish a clear decision-making process for when you do run into a challenge so a decision can be made quickly. List some examples of possible challenges and what the decision-making process should look like.

4. Since you know what you will measure, write a plan of action and include what will happen if a decision must be made or a challenge arises. These are some questions you can ask to help:

    ▶ Who will act in the roles you've laid out? _____

    ▶ This project/task _____ will start _____ and end _____. (You may need several of these statements for different parts of the project.)

    ▶ Where will actions occur? _____

    ▶ If you have a progress monitor/evaluator, then a reviewer, _____, will report on progress at _____ points in time.

6

Attention

"Give whatever you are doing and whoever you are with the gift of your attention."

—Jim Rohn

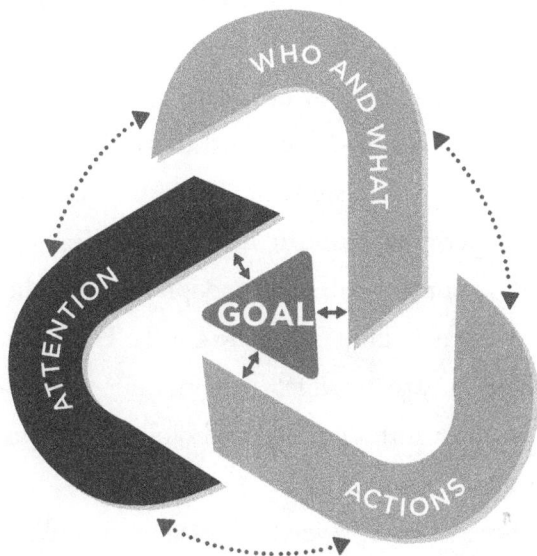

Have you ever watched a video with two teams of players passing basketballs among themselves, and you were asked to count the number of passes on one of the teams? It's difficult to track because of the number of balls going back and forth while the team members move around. This video was very popular in the early 2000s. If you haven't seen it, it goes like this: six people play basketball, three people on a team, passing around two basketballs simultaneously. Three team members are in white shirts and three in black shirts. Each team passes basketballs back and forth while moving. Your task is to count the number of passes made by the team in white shirts. Sounds easy.

When you are done counting, a facilitator asks, "Did you see the gorilla?" During the video, a gorilla strolls into the middle of the action, faces the camera and thumps its chest, and then walks away. When groups of people who didn't know about the gorilla were asked if they saw the gorilla, about 50 percent answered no.

When you see the gorilla, it seems remarkable that anyone could miss something so obvious. Two researchers, Christopher Chabris and Daniel Simons, developed this experiment at Harvard University when they were studying inattentional blindness. When they did the experiment—and it has been replicated hundreds if not thousands of times—half of the people who watched the video and counted the passes did not see the gorilla. For that subgroup of people, the gorilla was invisible. This invisible gorilla experiment is described in most introductory psychology textbooks and is featured in dozens of museums.

The experiment reveals several things about people. First, we can miss a lot of what goes on around us every day. Second, we don't even know we are missing so much around us. We do not have the opportunity to decide if we want to take any action or not because we just don't know that we have an opportunity.

Our minds don't always work the way we think they do. When we remember something, it may not be exactly as we actually saw it. You have likely had a disagreement with a family member or spouse in the retelling of some shared experience. If you are a fan of detective or police television shows, you know eyewitnesses are notoriously unreliable.

This final part of the model, attention, seems as if it would be straightforward. However, it is not. The constant flow of information and social media in today's world makes truly focused attention in short supply. In addition, the human tendency toward inattentional blindness compounds our awareness and attention to things and people. It's an ongoing subject of psychologists' studies because it is more prevalent than most of us think, and this chapter will hopefully help you find ways to reduce it and increase your attention to others.

I also discuss in this chapter different aspects of the word attention, which is the second most important part of the model after the goal. Even the simple act of listening is often not carried out with attention. Attention helps you recognize milestones and KPIs, check off a performance review, and give genuine appreciation. Attention encompasses all of these examples and more.

Attention in Collaboration

Attention is "the act or faculty of attending, especially by directing the mind to an object" (dictionary.com), and I add to this definition, "and another person." In my model for collaboration, attention also is monitoring, accountability, identifying problems, observing, adapting, improving, searching for people's talents, and acknowledging and celebrating milestones.

In the digital world, attention is more valuable than ever. We have to adapt the way we work with technology, not just adopt it and continue to maintain the same work patterns. With internet marketing, social network promotions, emails, and the news, to mention just a few, the noise is almost deafening. All of them are vying for your attention. Keeping your focus is key. Don't lose your attention because of digital notifications or the "next shiny object."

Technology cuts short the attention we give other people at times. It is easy and fast to send "thanks" in an email to someone who has worked hard and accomplished much. The speed with which we can communicate, using technologies, often makes us forget that the person on the receiving end might need a bit more than a five-second email. This especially applies to saying thanks in person. If said too many times without some feedback as to what specifically went well, you are missing an opportunity for both recognition and growth for the person receiving the praise.

Let's explore further how attention belongs in the model for collaboration. We make many decisions based on our perceptions, but our perceptions may not be the whole story. Quick judgements without clear observation of information can come back to bite us. For example, research has found that personal interviews for potential new hires may not be as effective as we think. They likely involve multiple biases on the part of those conducting the interviews. It might be we missed some of the things said, or we didn't like the way the candidate looked, or our minds wandered during that time. It might be that the questions we asked weren't as effective as we thought. What is striking is we may not know these were problems—another example of inattentional blindness.

ATTENTION

For effective collaboration, there is almost nothing more important than paying attention to what is happening and to the people involved. Paying attention is critical.

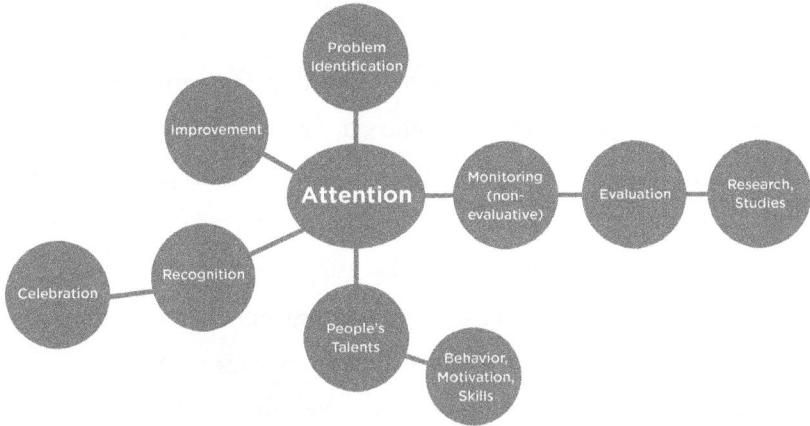

The diagram above illustrates most of the aspects of attention for this model. While attention isn't limited to these things, you can see that it encompasses a large number of aspects and therefore is important to the model for collaboration.

Pay Attention to Context

First, context determines how and why to apply your attention. The business ecosystem changes frequently. If you are not paying attention to what is going on, you potentially will be impacted before you're able to adjust. This concept is abstract, so let's look at the smallest type of collaboration and then a larger, more complex initiative.

At a team level, if the leader or the team is not paying attention, an aspect of the work is delayed and not shared with the team. On a strong team, when team members learn of what was missed, they adjust and keep moving. Often they are energized by solving a problem. At the same time, a team without a purposeful goal can get demoralized if they have to backtrack or do extra work. This can cause animosity and at worst, retribution to the person who let them down. A leader or the team members will need to raise the issue and discuss a solution. Many teams avoid conflict, but it is important to know conflict in itself is not bad. Conflict can bring a team closer if the issues are addressed rather than ignored, particularly if they see they are still moving forward toward the goal and not just placing blame. The leader should be looking at the big picture of the team's interactions, zooming out, while helping the team zoom in on the problem.

A strategy for catching and preventing behavioral issues is to create a team charter. Listing what behaviors your team will display as it is operating at a high level is very helpful. The list should include things like honesty, openness to ideas, feedback, listening, no meetings after the meeting, and conflict for resolution rather than the outcome the individuals desire. The charter should be personal for the team. Teams should put in words the way they will treat each other and make it visible for their regular meetings. And if there is a violation, one of the members—not just the leader—needs to call it out. This is attention in regard to team behavior.

At the organizational level, it is more complex, as the example of the team gets magnified due to all the teams working on the initiative. Remember the position types of a collaboration? Several of them were related to attention. They include Coordinating, Supporting, Overseeing, Testing, Evaluating, and Deploying. Having multiple positions that are responsible for attention helps ensure that things don't get overlooked.

Attention can begin with the leadership and teams, and then each division or department that might be involved. Any outside contractors, partners, suppliers, or alliances are also included. With all these positions and people, no one person can manage to pay attention to everything. Collaboration begins when there is interaction and shared responsibility for success across the participating people.

How to Improve Attention

Asking good questions, being open to ideas, listening, and being flexible are the foundational characteristics of paying attention. Start with the simple things. There will always be additional actions needed while the work is in progress. For example, asking good questions, selecting new team members who can fill the expertise gaps in the current membership, adjusting the plan, or celebrating a milestone. Let's go through these foundational aspects.

Ask Good Questions

An important skill for any leader is knowing how to ask questions and then listen—really listen. By asking open-ended questions, you give people the opportunity to explore ideas or explain their reasoning. Listen to the response and spark additional discussion. If done well, it also allows conversations to continue and explore the idea further. Good questions solicit new thinking and are not binary. Jim Collins, in his book *Built to Last*, wrote, "Instead of being oppressed by the 'Tyranny of the OR,' highly visionary companies liberate themselves with the 'Genius of the AND.'" This highlights the idea that either/or thinking does not open options but narrows the possibilities.

Here are some examples of how to phrase questions to encourage open thinking rather than limit it:

Open: If we continue to sell our products as they are, what is likely to happen?

Limiting: Should we continue to sell our products as they are, or start a new line of them?

Open: What are we missing?

Limiting: Are we missing something, or do we just need to work harder or differently?

Open: What might be the implications if we do (X) now to our current product line?

Limiting: What might be the implication if we do (X) now or cancel our current product line?

The questions that do not have an "or" assume that the person asking may not already have the right answer in their head. Instead, they explore alternatives. When exploring ideas, try not to look for confirmation of what you are thinking. That is not listening but simply being sucked into confirmation bias. Give time for the idea to be fully explored.

Who you ask questions of is also important. Today, it is almost imperative to ask your customers for their ideas. Coca-Cola learned this years ago when they famously launched New Coke. Doing little experiments with products before launching them is a more common way to ask questions and solicit feedback today. Social media opens up huge and new audiences for feedback. Savvy use of social media is a new skill for collaborating in the business ecosystem. Collaboration includes your customers too.

Some less obvious possibilities are to create groups or volunteer committees, podcasts, events, and other feedback loops. Groups can be formed online through a number of platforms. They need to be watched in order to align with the values of the company. Groups can be in person, such as clubs. These small events and planners may want to host a gathering or feedback loop to get customer feedback that wouldn't be collected through the current channels.

You might develop volunteer groups to test products. They receive the product to try out and can communicate what they think about it through any networks they already have. I know of an outdoor apparel manufacturer that does this. Utilize social media too. Having your customers involved is an opportunity for innovation, depending on your sector or product.

Be Open to Ideas

Thinking you have the answer to everything is not an effective strategy to get others to work with you. To hear what others are thinking, you must have an open mindset. There may be several ways to solve a situation and it helps if you practice thinking differently. Exploring those options both as a mental exercise or with a small test in reality helps you get more and better feedback.

Being innovative is key to adapting. There are companies that run thousands of experiments a year. Some examples include Google, Booking.com, and Netflix. Even in the retail space, Kohl's ran one about their opening hours. If you want to do this there are tools now available online or in Thomke's book *Experimentation Works*.

Innovation begins with asking questions internally and being open-minded to what the answers might be. These experiments are usually conducted in the short term and the results inform the next steps. Without them, a company's efforts for innovation or change can stall.

Listen

Listening well is probably a new leadership competency. It is a skill all leaders should do well. Listening is both easy and hard. For example, ask good questions and have an open mindset, but if you don't listen to feedback or the answers, it's futile. Often individuals, departments, or supervisors sink an idea because they think they know best. Building a culture of openness and listening is important for long-term success.

Really listening has two parts. The first is the act of hearing what is said without judgement. This may be the hardest thing to do. Checking your understanding is a strategy to bring more aspects of an idea out for greater understanding.

The second part is doing something about what you hear. This doesn't mean immediate action, but it could mean more research, getting feedback from others who are impacted, a mental exercise to imagine the implications, or a small experiment and trying out the idea. If you skip the second part, the culture of listening won't grow. Having multiple players on a team can be helpful in executing this, as they can take responsibility for the idea and test it out with their groups and bring the results back to the team.

Listening well also helps you identify when milestones are reached. Celebrating a milestone can go a long way to encourage more positive behavior. People like to be appreciated and acknowledged. It helps them feel connected and gives them a sense of how their role contributes to reaching the final goal. Leaders have to pay attention to know what and when to celebrate.

Be Flexible

Flexibility is about having a growth mindset. It is believing and acting in ways that demonstrate you are open to change. Being flexible is necessary to promote asking good questions, being open, and listening, all of which build a more positive collaborative culture.

ATTENTION

As a leader, flexibility is where you may need to step into the process. Encourage the team to try things or go in new directions. At these intersections of ideas and decisions, leaders can emerge.

Monitoring and Managing Attention

So far, I have not used the words monitoring, evaluation, or accountability in this chapter. They can often have negative connotations. They should not, but they do. By asking good questions, being open to ideas, listening, and being flexible, you are monitoring and, in some cases, evaluating. You are also holding people accountable. This approach is a positive method of leadership.

Formal evaluations can and should be conducted as a part of the experiments you do or as part of your research. They should be informative and become a part of the process rather than only being summative and the only source of evaluation.

Humans make evaluation more challenging. Things such as biases, oversight, and inattentional blindness get in the way. Because of the speed of work today, taking the time to assemble and reflect on information is rare. It's made more difficult because collaboration is complex, and it's not a linear process with one person at the top making decisions and others carrying out the decisions.

I was once a part of a multi-partner collaboration that worked with seven state university campuses and two campuses of the state community college system. Several mathematics and science faculty were interested in a large grant from the National Science Foundation. They were offering $7 million to increase the number of mathematics and science teachers in the state.

At the time, the three largest state university campuses were involved. These three universities graduated the most teachers, which was under 15 teachers annually in science and math. With this amount of money, we could accomplish big things.

Our proposal was ultimately funded. Quickly we had to create an oversight group from our organizing committee of seven people. The role was to identify the right people, recruit them, and ask good questions. The group was open to ideas, listened well, and was flexible. The membership of the oversight group increased and shrank with time as the work changed, and the group evolved as the work often required other skills or knowledge.

We conducted marketing research on where potential teachers might come from. Then we rolled out a recruiting plan, involving the admission offices and their staff to analyze data and collaborate with each other across the campuses. They had never done this before—they had always competed in the past. The outreach involved advertisements on the radio, at movie theaters, and other places where potential high school students could be found. Financial incentives were developed for students who considered going into a teacher preparation program.

At the same time, another group began developing a plan for existing students who were in science and mathematics classes and who might consider becoming a teacher. New campus-based groups formed to run gatherings, support programs, and provide experiences to engage potential teachers. Faculty who taught math and science and education classes were engaged in their own learning and development. The science and mathematics faculty were asked to say at least once to their students that they may want to think about teaching.

Lastly, practicing math and science teachers became engaged in a set of mentoring and support efforts for the potential students. You can see that these things could not have happened if one person was in charge. There were many connected leaders who acted in their arenas.

We ran into problems getting the schools to be supportive by giving the new practicing teachers a good training experience. To increase the numbers, we had to have buy-in from many new people. We shifted our strategy to provide new opportunities for faculty and schools. Part of it was money for activities, but our position was if they wanted good students in their classes, they should want good teachers.

New behavior was exhibited by the administration and faculty of these campuses, and others wanted to join. There were many little celebrations throughout the four years and at least one big celebration annually. The trust, communication, and flexibility of the group was amazing.

Through this initiative, we had an outside formal and informal evaluation. The formal evaluation was tightly controlled and we only had access to "findings" annually. At the same time, the informal evaluation conducted surveys, visited sites, and attended events to interview people. This data was regularly reviewed, which allowed us to adjust.

This collaboration was a combination of guided and hands-off support. The initial group of seven people continued through all four years, carrying the initial vision. They did not have direct control of much of what was happening. The students, faculty, and teachers all took individual and group action. At times it seemed like it was chaos, but there was more activity than the initial group would have been able to conceive themselves because we didn't know everything. The momentum increased and programming developed without the oversight group interfering.

Additional money was awarded to support the effort because of the successes. The result of the work was about a 250 percent increase in the number of mathematics and science teachers in three and a half years. Four additional state university campuses and two campuses from the state community college system joined in the effort after two years. That expansion occurred without any push from the oversight group.

This collaboration is still going on, although it has evolved. If you know anything about universities, you know they do not move very fast. We were able to accomplish much in a few short years.

This story illustrates that paying attention to the principles of collaboration works while measuring outcomes.

Problems in Collaboration

There are a few things to pay attention to during a collaborative project: competition among peers, team members waiting for approval by someone with decision-making authority, and moving too quickly.

Competition is necessary but not sufficient for moving things forward effectively. It is a stressor. A little stress is motivating, but too much crushes new thinking and possibilities. It can create internal competition among people and competition across departments or companies. If all the parties involved will benefit from collaborating, destructive competition will diminish. If the benefit is financial, it is even easier. If the purpose aligns with everyone's goals, there is less need for competition. For example, a focus on helping the community in some concrete way can energize a partnership.

Positive feedback, whether on an individual or organizational basis, can be a driver for forward motion. This can take the form of celebrations, which can be public or private. Paying attention to what is happening is key to getting this right. If you are too late to celebrate, then everyone has moved on. If you celebrate too early, the danger is not actually reaching the milestone you're celebrating.

ATTENTION

Simultaneous Wide and Narrow Focus

Paying attention requires a view that is both wide and narrow, a sort of constant zooming out and zooming in. It focuses on both the small and large aspects of a project, as well as on individuals, teams, and organizations. The more you pay attention, the better.

It seems contradictory to look wide and narrow at the same time. The wide view follows trends, whether they are in markets, consumers, incentives, or where a leader wants to go. These are likely things that don't have a concrete answer. But taking a risk with the information you currently have can help a company adapt, evolve, and change. It is an educated risk.

Think back to the university collaboration example. Admissions was key to the sustainability of our work at the faculty and school level. Without increasing the number of students in the education programs at some point, it would hardly matter to the pipeline if the numbers were in the single digits. It took us a year and a half to realize that was a weak link in the system. We had to understand what existed, who were the players, and who had influence to make things happen. We also realized few universities around the country were looking at how to do this. There were no examples of targeted recruiting approaches.

Paying attention to the details is easier because that is what most of us do. If you know where you are going, and you have KPIs or outcomes that are larger than tasks, then you can determine if the effort will get you to where you want to go. An example here builds from the admission problem. We had someone from one of the teams who noticed that at McDonald's restaurants, paper placemats often have advertisements on them. We wondered if we could benefit from this, so we asked.

McDonald's said yes and helped us promote our initiative and used it as an opportunity for McDonald's to get some good publicity.

We did not have to pay for the placemats as they could print them as a public service and get publicity from it. It seemed like a win-win. We dropped the program when surveys revealed none of the incoming freshmen had seen the placemats. Fortunately, we still used radio, movie theaters, and financial incentives, as those efforts were working.

In this case, the big picture was targeted recruitment, and the detail was looking closely at the tactic or program we used to target students.

Correcting Through Attention

If a manager or leader interacts with their team members regularly, issues, successes, and failures will come up, revealing whether team members are engaged in their work. Pay attention to individuals. Rather than providing a performance review, check in. You can use these questions to get started:

- ▶ What are you working on this week?

- ▶ What challenges do you foresee, and what support do you need or what can I do to help?

If after a couple of weeks these questions are answered quickly or with little effort, then it should catch your attention that they may be coasting and not challenged. Take a look at how they are interacting with others on the team, or ask others if they think the person has completed their role without being evaluative.

The leader can evoke the charter and ask the team member if they are enjoying the work. If so, why? Is there something else they would rather do? What feedback are they receiving from others about their work? Maybe there is something in their personal life that is going on. Maybe other team members are blocking them in some way. This process should look widely at outside factors to find out what is going on.

ATTENTION

Effective leaders have a combination of intuition and data to help them decide how to proceed if a team member is not engaged. Many times, just having the discussion with an employee can really change how they act for the positive.

In a traditional organization, there is a real problem when a team member is not interested or engaged in a project. In this traditional structure, the members do not change; they adjust to the new project and forge ahead. This is not a problem if you create a new team for each project; the individuals bring the strengths you need for the project. When the project is over, they may be distributed over other teams or to a new project.

If you know much about the movie-making business, they use this model to the extreme. For each film, they hire all new people, from actors down to the last sound person. When the filming is done, they let everyone go. This is one version of how the model can be applied. With my model for collaboration, the job is fitted to the people and the people to the job.

In small organizations, fitting this way is not always possible because there are fewer people to swap in and out. In that case, begin with hiring. Learn as much as you can about the behaviors, motivators, and competencies of the people you hire. Let them know they may not have the same position the entire time they are at the company. Don't waste the team's time with someone who is not interested and potentially poisonous to the rest of the team. Reassign them to other work that needs to get done and utilize them when they are ready and want to be there. When you keep the same people on a project, they can slow the process with their lack of enthusiasm. Pay attention to the people.

Employees have strengths. Using their expertise is better for your company and better for the employees' own satisfaction.

Reflection

Here are some questions to help you apply the attention component to your collaboration.

- ▶ What are your milestones and do they align with another team or department? By combining aspects of what you do with others, you might get better productivity.

- ▶ What do you have control over, and can you leverage that with another team or department?

- ▶ What are the attributes and talents that you need for this effort and can you find them among your employees?

- ▶ What milestones have you or your team achieved that could be celebrated?

- ▶ Ask your team what milestones you have missed and how do you make up for them?

- ▶ Assess the level of competition on your team or in your department. Is it destructive to the company's performance? By how much? And how would you know?

- ▶ What metric could you use that others would want to work together on, to increase the company's bottom line?

- ▶ Is the performance system you use rewarding individuals or teams? What aspects could you adjust?

- ▶ Are the awards given to individuals or teams? What are some team or collaborative effort awards that can be given?

7

The Parts in Action

"Science is built up of facts, as a house is with stones. But a collection of facts is no more a science than a heap of stones is a house."

—Henri Poincaré

How the Components Work Together

All collaborations are iterative with multiple people or groups doing work. You must be flexible to adjust the plan if circumstances change. Milestones should be set and followed to celebrate wins. While you must set specific targets to achieve, the path to get there is fluid. You know a collaborative effort is going well if the problems and challenges are mostly handled at the level where they arise, and if more people or organizations want to participate in the project.

While the model is not a step-by-step process, the components of the model do have a starting point and an ending point. These are unique to each project. You don't have to follow a particular sequence to build a collaborative project. The best order to address each component of the model depends on the context, business size, and project scope.

By now you realize the most important component of the model is the goal, the guiding star. It provides the purpose for participants and drives all aspects of collaboration. Attention is the next most important component, as it offers support and concludes milestones with celebrations. Both are needed for effort to be sustained and for the project to not break down.

The people and the plan can and should adapt as necessary. A small collaboration might be done in a month, while larger ones could take years. The structures needed to support a collaboration clear the way for work to happen and protect the effort from sabotage. It will take a shift in thinking about leadership and being a leader. This chart illustrates the shift that needs to occur.

A Leadership Shift	
Traditional Leader Stance	**Connected Leader Stance**
Hierarchical Organization/ Structures • Top down • Decision-making flows up • Organizational trees • Power is handed out	Organization as an Ecosystem • Fewer levels • Decision-making at many levels • Organizational matrix and trees • Many involved in planning
Directive Leadership • Command • Fear driven • Leader knows best	Many Leaders • Grey/contrarian • Networked leadership • Engagement driven • Serve others
Individualistic • Advance at another's loss • Maximize power • Individual as unit of measure	Inclusive • Advance based on group progress • Rewards teams • Teams as unit of measure
Extrinsic Motivation • Promotion • Financially focused • Want increased status	Intrinsic Motivation • Purpose • Want to give back • Help others
Competition • Win/lose • Growth only • Rewards individuals	Collaborative Competition • Win/win • Collaborate in one area, compete in another • Caring for each other
Exclusive and Few Decision-Makers • Leaders only • Have to check on decision-maker • Possessive of decision-making • Discrimination and bias	Diverse and Inclusive Decision-Making • Broad discussions • Decision at point of action • Sharing decisions and accountability • Watch for bias and correct
Blame • Not my job • It's their fault • Accountability and negative consequences	Attention • Monitor • Celebrate success • Test, maintain accountability, and learn

The Model in Action

Let's look at two examples of how the model works, one from the nonprofit sector and one from business. Remember that the parts themselves do not equal a working system. A system works because the parts work together in specific and intentional ways.

The Model in Nonprofit Organizations

A collaboration among four organizations, three of which were large and historically powerful in Washington, D.C., was destined to be a challenge. After months of negotiating and formulating a joint vision for a new project that was badly needed nationwide in the science education community, four national organizations were able to launch a transformative initiative that would reach students in grades K-12 across the country.

The vision was set. In one of the final organizing meetings to discuss the concrete steps for moving forward, one of the representatives said they were going to move forward alone. They would use emails and tell the other organizations what would happen and what role they may be able to play.

Months of discussions and planning stopped dead. We had outlined roles, strategies, and tactics for the effort. Was all this for naught? I felt I had to intervene, so I asked whether we had been doing all this planning and work as a partnership, or was something else going on?

What the representative of this group was suggesting was not a collaboration. The meeting became tense and then ended. A collision of ideas and values had occurred.

Prior to this meeting, none of the organizations had worked together before and one, as a matter of policy, did not collaborate or partner with other organizations. These organizations were not political organizations, but Washington, D.C., is a political place even for those not in politics.

The risks were high for all involved if any one of the players didn't follow through. Their reputations, money, and jobs could be on the line. The organizations included two national associations, one research group, and one technical assistance group. They represented millions of potential customers: organization members, states, educational systems, and researchers. The support and resulting revenue would be in the millions of dollars in the first couple of years and could last at least 10 years.

The immediate objective was the publication of one document while the ultimate goal that held the collaboration together was a new vision for science education in the country. The work would lead to additional support materials, professional training, certification research opportunities, course design, curriculum, and grant moneys all associated with this one document. The rollout of the project was critical to its success because without full support from the other organizations, the scope would not be realized. The size of the audience was huge. None of the four groups separately could reach all of the targeted audience or customers alone.

All of these organizations, except for one, had been searching and competing for funds to invest in this particular project. One funder was communicating with only one group because of their credibility. The other organizations were potentially going to have to decide to expend their own resources or drop the project.

What would you do? Walk away from the table? These are the types of questions that should be asked regularly when deciding on a partnership or collaboration and during a collaboration. Conflicts—or collisions, as discussed earlier—can result in better products or stronger partnerships, if people are willing to stay focused on the goal and work through the details. One way to do this is to ask whether this collaboration will leave a legacy or make the world better.

The collaboration decided we should go forward together with a slightly different resource allocation model, which was acceptable to everyone. The collaboration worked. Several national standards documents have been published, thousands of trainings have been offered nationwide to K-12 teachers and university faculty, many supplemental and resource books have been published, and conferences have focused on the topics from these visionary documents, across the country. The work we did in these areas still is going eight years after I left.

If the vision or goal is strong, then conflict should not sideline it. Collisions will happen, but it does not need to derail the effort.

The Model in Business

Here I will examine challenges and options that companies have run into to illustrate how they connect to the model. One company has seen revenues increase from $8 billion to $15 billion in eight years. The company is Stryker and they produce medical devices. They were benefiting from a growth of healthcare equipment needs, but they were also doing some unique things. The CEO talked about what they do every day in this way: "Innovation can only be derived if you're very, very closely collaborating with customers . . . We don't want to invent anything without iteration with our clinical customers."

The company has a decentralized structure that shares power and acquisition strategy throughout the organization, allowing it to be as close to the customer as possible. They utilize customers in their innovation process. Much of their growth has been due to collaborating and benefiting from close partnerships and mergers.

Their approach is to collaborate with their customers and allow them into the equipment testing process. This requires trust in the relationship so the customers do not tell others about the products since they are only in a testing phase. The company goes through an iterative process with their customers to refine the product.

This gives an advantage to those companies who can connect more quickly with customers and exposes vulnerabilities in companies that are physically based. The digital platform adds a new dimension to the word flexibility. While technology is not a savior for companies, it does provide new opportunities because of its flexibility and reach. As Greevan and Yu argue, it provides new competitive advantages because it allows you to reconnect with partners, maximize learning systemwide, explore new market capabilities, and rethink the customer problem (*Harvard Business Review*, 2020). Most of these advantages require collaborating with others.

How collaboration works as a larger success strategy, particularly in an economic downturn, can be seen from a set of data of various industries and their performance during and after the 2008 recession. The chart illustrates that those in a joint venture of some sort performed at a higher level than those wholly owned and controlled. A 2020 *Harvard Business Review* article by Bamford, Baynham, and Ernst cited data showing that the average return on assets across a wide range of industries was approximately 2 percent higher for joint ventures as compared to wholly owned and controlled entities. For example, in manufacturing, wholly owned entities averaged 4.5 percent while joint ventures averaged 6.5 percent.

What about collaborations in smaller companies? A small manufacturer that produces a product has the help of multiple suppliers. This company's collaboration is extended to their suppliers in the early development of a product. The company has to count on their suppliers to deliver the necessary parts on time. They depend on transportation systems to get the parts to their facility and from the facility to a distributor. Each of these companies might require a different platform for communication, making the initial phases difficult. Both partners will benefit in revenue if they collaborate to produce and distribute the product.

If one or more of the suppliers is not always as reliable as they might be, the company has to find another supplier to work with. If successful, this expands their capability to produce the product. All of these choices the company has made have components of the collaboration model. What's the goal, who can play, what role will they play, what actions will they take, and what monitoring will they need? If the new supplier fell short, could they go back to the original supplier? Could they source another supplier? This is one of the reasons to collaborate, because having multiple partners can be a type of protection from economic downturns or crises.

The Model in a Complex Ecosystem

The complexity of the model increases when more people or organizations are involved and when speed is needed. When do you make adjustments to ensure the collaboration can continue? How do you adjust to a changing market? Which partners will survive and change in the marketplace for their business? Paying attention to long-term and short-term factors is key.

Marketing and advertising have been transformed over the past two decades. An external communication approach today is multi-pronged across multiple platforms that keep changing. The messages also rapidly change because of the different platforms. Some companies partner with communication providers rather than hire new teams to keep up. This can be more successful if handled like a collaboration rather than a contractor. Research requires an expertise that some companies do not have. Companies that utilize other companies to do research can test and explore without larger commitments.

Below are some challenges that result in large-scale failures of a collaborative project:

▶ The goal is forgotten and the effort is reduced to benefit only a small group of individuals.

▶ Not enough attention is paid to the culture of the collaborators, and the people involved may not be acknowledged.

▶ Decisions are slowed by bureaucracy and people get impatient.

▶ Established metrics are ignored or the metrics measure the wrong things to start with.

These challenges can be mitigated by sticking to the principles of collaboration: trust, integrity, transparency, and sharing leadership. Remember *people* do the work. Helping people falls into the last part of the model, which is the attention component.

Here are some additional scenarios to illustrate problems where collaboration can be very helpful (Jones, 2012).

Example Situations Where Collaboration Is Needed	Typical Problems Observed
1. Team Building Across Boundaries Mergers, alliances, incubators	Roles and accountabilities are not clear; lack of cooperation
2. Cross-Functional Design Projects Working with experts from diverse backgrounds	Lack of cooperation; inability to communicate
3. Strategy Change and Realignment Redefine business model, improve market position, clarify vision	Confusion, concerns, and insecurity; lack of cooperation
4. Process De-Calcification Adapting to changing market conditions, updating "status quo" processes and practices	Apathy or resistance to change; lack of cooperation
5. Customer Service Improving customer service consistency, accountability, or overall performance	Inability to communicate; unclear roles and guidance
6. Organizational Change Realigning business processes to new leadership structure	Resistance to change; lack of cooperation

Any collaboration has more people involved in decision-making than a traditional reporting structure of leadership. In the planning phase, calculate for authority structures to be pushed down into the organization. One initial planning tool that might be helpful is the *collaboration canvas*. The modified version here was first developed by Ron Price as a part of the book *Growing Influence*. It can act as a place to sketch out your ideas and force you to think in multiple dimensions.

Collaboration Canvas

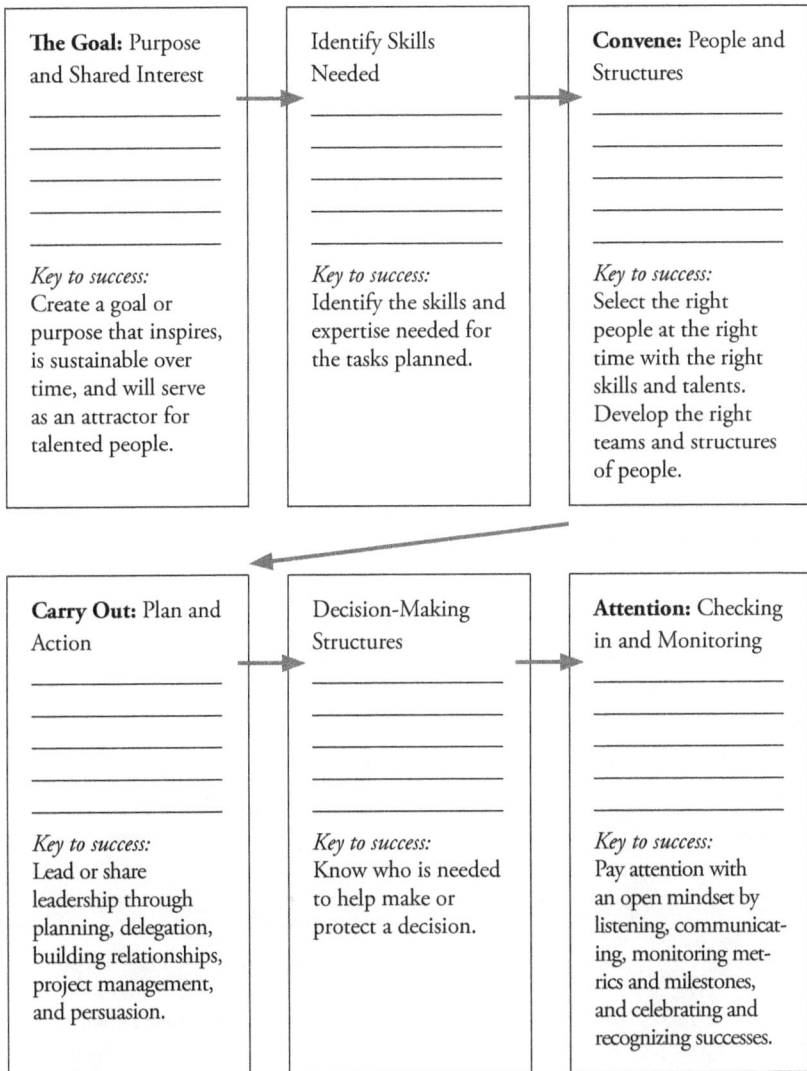

The Goal: Purpose and Shared Interest	Identify Skills Needed	**Convene:** People and Structures
_____ _____ _____ _____ _____	_____ _____ _____ _____ _____	_____ _____ _____ _____ _____
Key to success: Create a goal or purpose that inspires, is sustainable over time, and will serve as an attractor for talented people.	*Key to success:* Identify the skills and expertise needed for the tasks planned.	*Key to success:* Select the right people at the right time with the right skills and talents. Develop the right teams and structures of people.

Carry Out: Plan and Action	Decision-Making Structures	**Attention:** Checking in and Monitoring
_____ _____ _____ _____ _____	_____ _____ _____ _____ _____	_____ _____ _____ _____ _____
Key to success: Lead or share leadership through planning, delegation, building relationships, project management, and persuasion.	*Key to success:* Know who is needed to help make or protect a decision.	*Key to success:* Pay attention with an open mindset by listening, communicating, monitoring metrics and milestones, and celebrating and recognizing successes.

This collaboration canvas is a simplified way to see all the parts together. I am hopeful it will provide you a launch pad for your collaborative work.

Reflection

How are you looking at your project? Do you have a wide and narrow view? Test out the collaboration canvas and sketch in your responses for each of the boxes in the canvas.

The Goal: Purpose and Shared Interest	Identify Skills Needed	**Convene:** People and Structures
_____ _____ _____ _____	_____ _____ _____ _____	_____ _____ _____ _____
Key to success: Create a goal or purpose that inspires, is sustainable over time, and will serve as an attractor for talented people.	*Key to success:* Identify the skills and expertise needed for the tasks planned.	*Key to success:* Select the right people at the right time with the right skills and talents. Develop the right teams and structures of people.

Carry Out: Plan and Action	Decision-Making Structures	**Attention:** Checking in and Monitoring
_____ _____ _____ _____	_____ _____ _____ _____	_____ _____ _____ _____
Key to success: Lead or share leadership through planning, delegation, building relationships, project management, and persuasion.	*Key to success:* Know who is needed to help make or protect a decision.	*Key to success:* Pay attention with an open mindset by listening, communicating, monitoring metrics and milestones, and celebrating and recognizing successes.

8

Be an Infinite Learner

"Cultural analysis is intrinsically incomplete. And, worse than that, the more deeply it goes the less complete it is. It is a strange science whose most telling assertions are its most tremulously based, in which to get somewhere with the matter at hand is to intensify the suspicion, both your own and that of others, that you are not quite getting it right. But that, along with plaguing subtle people with obtuse questions, is what being an ethnographer is like."

—Anthropologist Clifford Geertz, 1973

I had the opportunity to spend the day with two people at Root & River who assisted me with developing or reshaping my personal brand. At first, I was unsure what a personal brand was and whether I really needed one. I knew who I was, and I thought other people knew as well. During this time, the Kardashians were at the peak of their social media stardom. They were the example of how to create a business with a personal brand. I was obviously behind the times.

We started very casually with my history, passions, and goals, and it became clear to me that this was a useful activity. They drew a life and career path from what I said. This helped identify what drove me to do what I did at work and in my life. We explored my authentic self. I had a revelation that I'd concealed for years much of who I was—someone with dyslexia—at work for fear of others' perceptions of me. Perhaps I wanted them to judge me by how I performed, and not where I came from or by my disability.

It struck me that I gained meaning from my work and personal life by helping others. In reflection, my career was never about the next position or title even though I've had many. I want to impact others. My career positions as a teacher and leader in nonprofits and businesses provided me with new ideas I could use as opportunities for others.

Move With the Ecosystem

We are all learners. We learn in different ways, but some people, like me, are infinite learners. Do you learn in one area or multiple areas? Some say it is of great value to be a generalist rather than focusing on one thing and becoming an expert in just one area. Steve Jobs felt this. This challenges the idea that the route to excellence is through specialization. In the book *Range: Why Generalists Triumph in a Specialized World*, David Epstein argues that flexibility in thinking and embracing new learning experiences is helpful and may be hard. You are not what you study in school or elsewhere, and it is okay to be wrong. Having others help is the key to success (Epstein, 2019). Where do you fit on the learning continuum?

Answer some of these questions to explore what type of learner you are and whether learning drives you.

▶ How many times have you changed jobs or positions?

▶ How many people do you know who have changed jobs multiple times? Do you know anyone who completely changed careers or started a new career?

▶ Do you read books regularly and watch documentaries or other informational videos?

If you answer yes to these, you may be an infinite learner.

When I started working, my perception of a career was that you didn't change jobs frequently, and if you did there must be something wrong.

Early in my career I developed about a four-year pattern for staying in a job. At the time I often said to myself, people must think I am flaky for changing jobs so frequently. Changing jobs is common but was not as much when I started working. Today the average person between the ages of 18 and 52 will change jobs 12.3 times (U.S. Bureau of Labor Statistics, 2019). There was a time when ambitious people thought of their career as something they would begin in their 20s or 30s, depending on how much schooling they needed, and then emerge about 40 years later as a person ready to retire. How many people do you know who took this path? This idea of one career has pretty much faded into history. Yes, there are some people who follow this path, such as teachers or healthcare workers. Even then, they may change positions within the field. With the gig economy, people today work for many companies and they may change jobs annually.

In the podcast *Worklife* by Adam Grant, a professor of organizational psychology at the Wharton School of Business at the University of Pennsylvania, he talks about frequent job changing and the "follow your passion" advice in so many graduation speeches. He says "follow your passion" is not great advice for younger people, since they may not really know what their passion is.

The venerable Peter Drucker encouraged trying many kinds of work while you are under 50 years old to help you build experiences that allow a more dynamic view of the world, or what might today be known as a full-spectrum mindset. An example might be thinking of consumers as people rather than labeling them as buyers of products. Thinking of them as people allows for a wider understanding of who they are, their identities, how they change based on age, location, and friends, and how that connects us as people rather than separate identities (Johansen, 2020).

Angela Duckworth, founder and CEO of Character Lab, a nonprofit whose mission is to advance the science and practice of character development, is a professor of psychology at the University of Pennsylvania. She is known for developing the concept of "grit." Rather than following your passion, she recommends you sample jobs when you are young, almost like dating. This way you will get a better sense of the expectations in a field and what you like. Being curious allows you to develop your passion, and sometimes you need to develop enough competence in something to develop a passion for it. Learning from the jobs you experience helps you decide what is a good fit for your goal.

Learn from your failures and your successes. John Gardner, in *Living, Leading, and the American Dream,* says when you hit a spell of trouble, ask, "What is this experience trying to teach me?" The lessons aren't always happy ones, but how you deal with them is important because they will keep coming. Take advantage of them.

As I mentioned earlier in the book, a local independent radio station I enjoy has an advertisement that ends with "Be a nerd, not part of the herd," noting that they are different from the larger commercial stations. This resonates with me because being different is not a bad thing. Conforming is rarely a good strategy.

A learning mindset or full-spectrum mindset is about being open to new or divergent ideas and trying new things. There are many ways to achieve this mindset, such as through diversity or connecting with people outside the company or team. Outsiders can provide critical pieces of information. They know things that can boost your business' performance.

Learners are more intrinsically motivated than externally. They want to build their own competencies and are more likely to pursue them on their own rather than from a suggestion from a manager or company.

Resilience and Flexibility

In the complex business ecosystem, and even in our daily lives, being resilient and flexible are important skills to keep pace with the world.

Resiliency is an important trait to help you withstand a variety of challenges. When you make mistakes and then deal with the emotional repercussions, you come back with new knowledge. The more this happens, the more you will learn. No one likes failure, but that is one way to build resiliency and flexibility. Another is to travel and cope with being in a country that does not speak your language. You could also collect feedback from your peers, and ask them about your performance. Handling criticism and learning from it is an expression of resiliency.

Flexibility is the ability to adapt to changes and handle situations in multiple ways. We can't know the future, so we create plans. Sometimes we make a plan B, C, and even D with contingencies. These alternative plans allow for flexibility when the factors that make plan A viable change.

To build flexibility, there are many things you can do. One is to look at things from another perspective. Become a "fly on the wall" to a discussion of a problem, and imagine if you were in their shoes what you would do. Be comfortable with ambiguity. Having an answer, even if it is not *the* answer, may be good enough. Adapting to change forces you to be flexible, and to be flexible, you have to be open to new ideas.

One of the best ways to build flexibility is by changing jobs. You meet new people, learn to operate new hardware and software, and learn the local office culture. Travel can also force you to be flexible, because no matter how well you plan, you will be thrown into an unpredictable situation that will force you to work through the changes.

Generations

The general workforce today has three or four generations of employees spanning 50 years. This provides a terrific opportunity to exchange ideas and have collisions of ideas. A lot has happened in 50 years and the way work can be done has changed. Even though people of the same generation are likely to want to work together, it is not ideal. Some people make assumptions about others based on their age or generation, but most differences are more of an individual characteristic rather than a generational one. What can we do to leverage the strengths of different generations in a collaboration? Think in terms of systems, interpersonal relations, and continuous improvement, and choose individuals based on skills rather than age. Who is a great thinker about how the systems work or could work? Who is good at communicating and connecting with everyone? And who has talents for metrics and measurement?

Learn How to Learn

To collaborate effectively, it's helpful to understand how you learn. I never wondered about why I like books so much while other people seem to reject them. As I began to probe, I learned that some people don't value text as much as I do. This was curious to me. Unfortunately, I don't have the time to read all the books I'm interested in, so I have been adapting to use audiobooks and podcasts. This is something I know about myself. I am on the extreme end of the scale of motivation to learn. Wherever you are on the spectrum of liking books, you are still a learner. The people who do not read may still value learning but in different ways, such as through experience. YouTube has been helpful for many people because you can find videos to teach you almost anything.

To understand more about your preferences for learning, you can take a motivator assessment. The TTI Success Insights motivator assessment is one I find particularly helpful. They have a continuum in a category they call "knowledge." On one end of the continuum are instinctive learners and on the other are intellectual learners. I fell high on the intellectual end. I have a friend who is quite high on the instinctive learner end of the continuum. He says he doesn't like to read. He is actually a quick learner and can remember most of what transpired in a conversation. The books he has are mostly about how to be more effective at his work. He is a learner, but he learns differently from me. He is an on-demand learner, to fulfill a need. These are extremes and most people are somewhere in the middle of the continuum.

To increase your learning, become more deliberate about learning by developing a learning plan. Workplaces have performance improvement plans, but how common are learning plans for employees? Learning plans can be short term or long term. Obtaining an advanced degree would be a part of a long-term plan. Developing a new skill or technical knowledge would be a part of a short-term plan. Employees can create a learning plan based on what they want to accomplish. This might include networking, finding a mentor, or taking courses. The idea is to map out a way to achieve personal learning goals. The importance of developing a plan is very often pushed aside in the busyness of work and life. You have to be deliberate if you want to grow.

Another way to force yourself to learn is to change your context. Learning happens when you stretch yourself beyond what you're comfortable with. Some people thrive on change and require it to be innovative. Barry Diller, former CEO of Paramount Pictures, founder of Fox Broadcasting and creator of the first TV movies and miniseries, on Reid Hoffman's podcast *Masters of Scale* discussed how he changed jobs purposefully even when he had achieved C-suite status. The changes he made were dramatic. He values knowing little about the new businesses he jumps to. He then has a naive view about the company and can ask a lot of questions. Because he is an instinctive learner, he learns from experience and applies that knowledge to his work. He listens carefully and synthesizes the knowledge to craft new or different solutions.

As a leader, if you got to where you are by your expertise, this might seem like a crazy thing to do. What if questions, even stupid ones, leveraged people with the expertise to look at things differently? To be a leader who learns, you have to have humility and look to others who might know more than you for many situations. When working with other companies such as partners, suppliers, or contractors, it is helpful to be open to their ideas and listen. Their experience and knowledge is likely different from yours and it is to your advantage to learn from them.

Responding with an anecdote about how you had a similar experience is not as effective as just listening. Create a bond by taking a nonexpert stance—this strategy is disarming. If you do push your experiences, you can be seen as competitive. It devalues what they are telling you. A colleague I greatly appreciate, Ron Price, uses the phrase, "There is a treasure inside every person. You just have to take the time to find it."

Strive to create learning opportunities in meetings. Effective meetings are those where you learn, new ideas are exchanged, and problems are identified and sometimes solved. Making clear the structure, time, purpose, scope, and whether a decision is needed can be helpful for people to be effective in meetings. Building in time for comments opens opportunities for more learning. Typically a few people dominate meetings. All attendees need to know their ideas will be valued and probed for further understanding. A leader might be quiet, listen, and facilitate.

Technology has made information and learning so much more accessible. Working professionals increasingly show a desire to learn using technology. According to a 2019 article by Deb Jewell, up to 60 percent of working professionals would consider online learning because it is convenient and flexible.

There are many options now available for traditional courses, hybrid courses, or small chunks of content. The impact of learning through an online environment is not well documented, but these resources are great to fill in the content gaps in a learning plan.

Coming back to the idea of a learning plan, creating one is straightforward. Identify the skills you want to learn, then assess how far you have to go and determine which course, book, online skill builder, podcast, or other instructional material will help you most. Another approach is to learn from another person and work closely with a mentor. If you're an experiential learner, you could ask for a transfer to another position within the company. Determine what you need to do to acquire the skill based on your learning style.

Use the following structure to develop a learning plan or use the canvas in the reflection section:

1. My goal:

2. Skill(s) or position I want:

3. Timeline (by when):

4. Who can help me:

5. Program or position I'll learn from:

6. Milestones I will acknowledge:

Reflection

To build your capacity for learning, make time to create a plan. Without this step it will likely be much harder. Think about the following questions or use the planning canvas.

- ▶ What do you want for your future? (your goal)

- ▶ What are a few steps you can take now to start getting there? (people and plan)

- ▶ How do you learn best: reading, talking with others, experiencing, or physically rehearsing?

- ▶ Have you tried visualizing your future? (Athletes often visualize how they will perform in an event and even the steps they take through the competition.)

- ▶ What steps can you take first? (plan)

Use your answers to develop a plan. You may start with a short-term plan to prepare you for your longer-term goal.

Now that you have a plan, act!

Below is a canvas to help you think through your answers to the questions above.

The Future

What do you want for your future?

Your Goal

Translate your aspiration into a goal. For example, "I want to be a VP" would translate to "I want to increase my leadership skills to be promoted every few years." Your goal:

Skill and Knowledge

What skills and knowledge do you need?

Who Can Help?

Write the names of people you can talk with who could help you better understand the goal/role you are seeking.

How Do You Want to Learn?

Do some research and list here the ways you can grow your skills and knowledge, including a mentor if that is possible.

Timelines and Logistics

What steps do you need to take and by when?

What permissions will you need to pursue this?

9

Getting Lost

*"It finally happened. I got the GPS lady so confused, she said,
'In one-quarter mile, make a legal stop and ask directions.'"*

—Robert Breault

One of the most exciting things about running a business or organization is that opportunities abound. You have heard stories of a company that wants to expand into other services or products, and it goes badly. One example could be Sears. A story where it worked out, although rocky, was GE.

Both companies are still around. One is more successful than the other. Sears was a retail giant. Their mission today is "to grow our business by providing quality products and services at great value when and where our customers want them, and by building positive, lasting relationships with our customers." They expanded into many other types of offerings over the years, from homes to financial services. Originally, they were a mail-order company. If they had stayed focused on their core mail-order service, imagine where they would be if they'd gone to online selling at the right time? Amazon before Amazon?

GE is another story. They have made so many different products over the years, if I ask you what they sell now, you may not know. They have been in the industries of electric incandescent lights with Thomas Edison, electric locomotives, X-ray machines, radio broadcasting, electric appliances, vacuum tubes, television sets, moldable plastics and compounds, commercial jet engines, nuclear power, laser lights, and medical devices. This may be why it is hard to say what they do. They have had good leadership and have made it through a number of rocky mergers and spinoffs. They still have strong credibility and a viable business.

Why do I use GE as an example when they obviously didn't stick to a core product? Actually, they have done pretty well with sticking to their core mission. Their mission statement today is "to become the world's premier digital industrial company, transforming industry with software-defined machines and solutions that are connected, responsive, and predictive."

With this mission as their guide, they have flexibility, and while it may seem they are all over the place, they are innovating in providing services for businesses and consumers. It is important to remember what your business is so you don't get lost.

Stay Observant

Have you ever used a GPS in your car to navigate to a location you had never been to? When you got there, did you wonder exactly where you were? What is worse is when you have to travel back to where you started without it.

Having moved several times in a two-year period, I used my GPS a lot to get to places, particularly in urban centers. Oddly, even when I was able to get to the location, it was rare that I had confidence in where I was in relation to other things. If anyone asked me to reverse my steps without the GPS, I wouldn't be able to do it.

The GPS encourages you to look at the immediate road ahead and the screen, without paying attention to much else. What you miss—or at least I did—are landmarks such as gas stations, churches, intersections, stores, unique structures, train tracks, or houses. Sometimes you don't even notice the traffic. The reference points we use to help us remember the way don't exist because we follow directions rather than seeing where we're going.

Having reference points and landmarks is much more than sightseeing—it is noticing the things around you and observing. Observing is a critical skill for a leader. What do you know about the people immediately around you and the people throughout the company? When you talk with them, are you learning new things about their lives and family or only doing business? What life landmarks can you use to connect with them?

Connect with the people on your team and observe how they interact. The better you know them, the better able you are to observe and see subtle differences. Paying attention gives you better clarity about their strengths, allowing you to notice when something is wrong. This applies beyond the people in your company.

When working with people, teams, partners, and collaborators, people are unlikely to agree on many things. To apply the model for collaboration, you must be open-minded, make mistakes, support others, and be willing to give up some control. That is learning in real time.

If you're aware of their struggles or challenges, it is helpful to advancing your combined purpose, because when you know, you can act.

Personal Derailment

As you stay observant, pay attention to your internal emotions and ideas that can derail you and your efforts. We carry our emotions in ways that we think are hidden, but they are often observable. Both positive and negative emotions are like a contagion in that they can spread.

Sigal Barsade, an expert on contagions and culture, says an emotional contagion is when we literally infect other people's emotions. Our emotions can be felt by others even when we are consciously trying to express very different emotions.

Let's say you have been trying to close a deal for six months and you finally do. You are ecstatic. Later that day, you go into a meeting with a person you have to let go. The positive feeling you have will be felt by that person even if you are trying to be serious. It will seem weird to them or they may think you are not a caring person.

The same is true with negative emotion. A conflict you have with someone will carry into your next meeting. Your negative emotions will be felt by others. When you observe others, look to see what else may be going on for them that day or in their personal lives.

Another type of emotion that may affect your leadership is one many leaders experience. You may be caught in a loop of self-doubt or self-criticism. This doubt is sometimes called "imposter syndrome." Think of it this way: we often don't feel we belong in a position because we believe we are not good enough. Every leader experiences this and there are times when it is appropriate to let others know your feelings to help solve the problems that weigh you down. It makes you vulnerable, which can help build trust.

Another potential difficulty is having a static mindset rather than a growth mindset. Ask yourself whether you're observing or just seeing. What are your strengths? When you emphasize them, are your able to increase your own influence to engage others?

Please note emotions and cognitive processing are factors that can derail us. Self-awareness of emotions and mindset are helpful to avoid allowing others to derail you.

Technology and Focus

Take the time to observe how people work with technology in your company or on your team. How do people use the company's systems and processes? Are you able to retrieve needed data easily such as performance, CRMs, and communication systems?

Technology systems can frustrate employees and cause negative reactions and emotions. Are your systems easy to use? Are there complaints from inside or outside the company about how they work? As a leader, you can do so much good by helping people do the work they want to do, particularly if it is being slowed or blocked by existing systems.

If you don't observe and learn, you are destined to be blind to many people and systems. You'll need crutches to get through the workday, just like we need GPS apps to help us navigate. We used the technology to get things done, but at what cost? When the people become frustrated by it, it slows down our workflow, or it distracts us from observing our surroundings.

Sometimes technology does solve our problems. I continue to use a GPS to get places. I know I don't always learn the route, but when I don't use the GPS I get lost. When I have time, I try to see what is around me.

I do embrace new technologies that make my life more effective. I didn't say more efficient because effective and efficient are very different things: Some things make my life efficient at the expense of connecting with people. A pitfall with any technology is it can seem to help but it may actually limit your human interactions. Have you ever stood in a grocery self-checkout line and had to wait and wait because people in front of you were unable to make the technology system work for them? They have to wait for a human to come and help them. The idea behind the self-checkout is it lowers cost because you don't need a cashier, and it helps shoppers check out more quickly. I am not sure it has accomplished either goal.

Leaders sometimes depend on the benefits of technologies to the detriment of people. Email, internal communication systems, multi-user project management tools, and video communication platforms are terrific help. Most of these applications are to assist people talking to other people. Even though they increase efficiency, they aren't a substitute for the human interaction, the face-to-face communication for relationship building.

People still do most of the work. You probably have had the experience of back-and-forth emails taking a great deal of time. If you had just called and talked with them, you could have had the conversation in five minutes. The ubiquitous nature of software can cloud our judgement about the most effective way to communicate with other humans.

The digitization of companies will continue to happen. Again, I am not advocating against using these tools. They allow us to do many remarkable things. My concern is expressed more clearly by Mark Johnson in his 2019 *Harvard Business Review* article, "Digital Growth Depends More on Business Models than Technology." He addressed a concern about the replacement of people by technology.

He described how the digitization of Dominos was successful and why other companies failed with their digitization process. Dominos' transformation was a game-changer, but the technology was not what changed its game—it facilitated it. They strengthened their cost volume profit by adding more convenience for customers and associates and more fun for people. They also upgraded their resources and processes needed to support their people. Customers and employees were part of their digitization calculus and they saw the benefit. Always consider with an existing or new technology whether it promotes or limits the interactions of people inside and outside the company.

I had a coaching a client once who was trying to figure out why their team members weren't interacting much during their team meetings. I asked how often they met, and did he meet with each member of the team individually and together as a group? The silence was all the message I needed to understand the situation. The client said they used email mostly to communicate and hence the team met once a month and sometimes those would be postponed. They perceived email as a fast and easy way to communicate.

Do you suppose a leader before email was invented would not meet with their people? This is an example of how a ubiquitous technology was used for its efficiency without thought about the impact on the people and their effectiveness. Fortunately, the client began to meet with their team members and delegate some tasks, and the team members became more involved and began working to solve problems and ask questions.

Project management systems are a good example of great tools to increase effectiveness. At the same time, tools like this can end up causing more problems if they are too complicated to use easily.

Team collaborative applications are a $3.5 billion dollar industry and expected to grow. What is interesting is these systems don't seem to have replaced email, which was the intent. Most people use both systems, though email use has declined a bit. They are large time consumers because to read and respond to a message, there is a several-step cognitive process. You have to decide to read the message, then if you do, do you respond? If you respond, what do you say? If you don't read it or respond, you need to decide when will you read it and respond. And where do you put the message? When you see who it is from or the topic, what emotional baggage is with you after reading it: positive or negative? You can think of it this way: the new productivity technology should be something you use less than the thing you used before.

All of this mental processing seems very quick, so no big deal, right? But you have lost focus from your original work. Not to pick on Slack, but it is a prevalent application, so its impact has been studied. If you get 30-50 Slack messages in an eight-hour day, it is virtually impossible to have much focused work time. It can take up to 23 minutes to get refocused on the task you were working on once distracted by an email or Slack message. It can take even longer to get to a mental "flow state" or what is called "deep work."

The interruption of focused work leads to trying to find more time in a day to finish work or leaving work feeling like nothing was completed. This feeling of incompleteness or bringing the work home interrupts any sense of work-life balance. And we know workplace software doesn't stay at work. Our minds, biologically, are just not meant to operate by being constantly interrupted. Frequent technology distraction has been linked to shorter attention spans, lower IQ, and increased levels of anxiety and depression, with an overall decline in work productivity (Wilmer, Sherman, and Chein, 2017).

One solution is changing company culture. Another is training employees to turn off those notifications and schedule time to check them.

To use technology to improve rather than substitute your leadership, here are some questions you can ask and things to do:

1. How will the tool/app help me promote connections or interaction with and among the people in my company and/or with our customers?

More than one client has told me that the primary way they interacted with their team was through email. When they did hold meetings, the staff weren't engaged and often missed performance benchmarks. Casual "in the hall" interactions, one-on-one check-ins, and formal meetings increase interactions. Ask your team what ideas they have to do their work better. Create sub-team groups to solve specific problems. Use email only for periodic updates, an article, or report—the things that aren't time sensitive.

2. In what ways does the app/tool build more opportunities for my team to observe the processes or important functions people are carrying out? Does the technology limit perspectives? Like a GPS mapping program, does it limit the big picture?

Performance management systems limit perspective. If goals, key performance results, and comments are the only information used for weekly, monthly, annual, or biannual performance reviews in the system, then it is limiting your opportunities for understanding the whole person. More regular feedback opportunities and performance check-ins are more effective. Effective teams are supported by leaders who know about the day-to-day successes and challenges. A leader can walk around talking with their people, listening, asking questions, and providing feedback. Even using short meetings for quick decisions and actions brings people together.

Often, I hear a reluctance to meet with a team because so much time is wasted. This is a shame as meetings don't have to be like that. We all have memories of endless meetings with no action at the end.

> **Effective meetings improve communication and save time over technologies that are best used for less complex communications.**

There are terrific project management tools that are very helpful for one or more people to track tasks, people, milestones, and time. However if those tools become a substitute for person-to-person check-ins, informal discussions, and formal meetings, leaders will miss the backstory, potential challenges, and opportunities that take too much time to write about—and they will make no human relationships or connections. With too much focus on accomplishing the numbers, leaders and team members miss opportunities to move faster and more effectively by being in touch with each other and to have support ready when it is needed.

3. How does the app/tool help with time-sensitive concerns?

When work is moving fast and you need responses quickly, consider which communication tool is best to get an answer. Emails may not be read quickly, texts might get misinterpreted, and long internal platform discussions can be tricky to follow. If you are in the same office, walk to their office. If not, call them.

Checking in informally is a great way to get a pulse about what is happening and make a human connection. You can call someone and share your ideas in 15 minutes or less. How does that compare to the other methods listed here? If something is time sensitive, walk or use the phone if possible.

Keeping technological tools in perspective can free up time for you and reduce stress. Sending an email and then waiting for a response builds stress, particularly if you are home. Direct contact is faster. I believe staying attentive to preventing technology from lulling you into complacency or increasing your stress is a good use of time. Use those supports that allow you to increase your focus and productivity while not sacrificing connections to other people. It may require building in "people time" to your day.

Mission Creep

Another type of distraction is mission creep. When resources are scarce and capacity is at its limits, how do you relieve the pressure?

One way is to expand into another area or merge to bring resources and capacity, and ultimately revenue. While I am a believer in looking for opportunities, the danger is in going beyond your ultimate goal or purpose. "Mission creep" is a term that comes from the nonprofit world, and it refers to the actions many nonprofits take when a funder or an opportunity is apparent—they accept it and add on a new service. The organization's mission is stretched so the purpose is no longer as clear. Mission creep applies to business too. Watch where you're going and ensure you do not lose focus.

The best way to not get too distracted is to remind yourself, your team, and your organization of your goal and purpose. If a new idea comes up, ask how it is related to your purpose. As a leader, reminding the employees why they are there and the role they play is an ongoing process. No matter when the leader talks, they should tie the actions being taken back to the goal or mission. Always ask what is the purpose and how does this idea advance or benefit the purpose?

Organizational Silos

Another way you can get separated from your vision is through organizational silos. The American Management Association reported from a recent survey that 83 percent of executives said silos existed in their companies and 97 percent thought the silos had a negative effect.

There are different types of silos: operational, channel, and hierarchical. Purpose can get lost in these silos, demotivating employees.

The *operational silo* is a functional silo where departments do not connect to each other within the company. A simple example might be the design department isn't connecting with marketing. A big advertising campaign is launched by marketing when the product isn't quite ready. Customers get excited and make orders and have to wait longer than expected. This affects the customer service department, who potentially have not been aware of the product launch. Customers get turned away, affecting the reputation of the product and company.

You may have seen these types of problems arise in your organization. Early communication and establishing purpose is an easier fix than trying to clear up the aftereffects of a mix-up.

The *channel silo* is a customer touch-point silo where external communication mechanisms don't match up or duplicate each other. As new channels for communication are developed, old ones are not necessarily eliminated. For example, what are the channels we use to communicate? Retail materials, print and catalog mailings, phone, mobile, website, television, cable, email, and various social media formats. An example of where communications can get crossed is when traditional channels are overseen by one group and newer channels by another group. The messages can get confused and this frustrates customers. The American Management Association survey reported that over 650 companies found that companies are trying to integrate these systems, but only 26 percent of them have a well-developed strategy. Most are a long way from an integrated strategy.

The *hierarchical silo* is another organizational silo, similar to operational silos in that people or teams aren't connecting and collaborating. It may be caused by promotion structures or titles. An example might be a manager who limits their team's actions because the manager must ask permission for each expenditure. In another case, a team could start solving a problem but they are not aware of the solutions that another group is working on because they don't connect across departments. Or a team of leaders may not connect with each other because they see it as a competitive disadvantage to do so.

These silos are up and down and across the organization. They may be seen in the organizational charts or as a result of reorganization, but more often this occurs because of how people work and respond to where they are located in the organization. A team leader could take advantage of their authority, or a team member could go around their team leader and cause problems. Sometimes these are behavioral concerns or communication problems, and other times the silos are structural.

I want to highlight through these examples that it is easy to get lost in details, structures, politics, and even egos with a collaboration, particularly when you involve technology and people from other organizations. It starts with the question of "Who is in charge?" These distractions diminish employee efforts toward the larger goal. Without an understanding of the individuals, the group, and the whole system, it is hard for a leader to lead with bold vision. A leader can get drawn into the day-to-day concerns, zooming in, and lose their way. The advantage of leading is enhanced by using their power of observation and looking for patterns and differences. Setting up structures for collaboration and reducing barriers helps you build in the goal from the beginning.

Leaders should take time to listen, observe, reflect, and then respond. Through listening instead of getting into the weeds, the leader is less susceptible to immediate distractions. Through reflection, they keep their observational lens open wide and are able to respond with fuller knowledge of what is going on and how it affects people.

Reflection

To not get lost, remember your purpose. Observe your own behavior around distractions and do not get pulled in. Ask yourself the following questions to better understand your tendencies and potential opportunities:

- ▶ Do you stay focused, or are you easily distracted with new ideas and suggestions?

- ▶ When a new idea or solution is suggested, does this idea further your goals or is it just a new idea?

- ▶ Do you have a way to monitor new ideas, prioritize, and try them in small experiments before jumping on board?

- ▶ How does your priority system help your team decide which ideas to pursue and which to sideline for later?

- ▶ How do you encourage someone on your team to always ask questions and challenge ideas to keep from losing sight of the goal?

- ▶ How do you prevent yourself from being the one who slows ideas from being implemented and slows progress toward the goal?

- ▶ What are the potential partnerships or collaborations you should start?

- ▶ What partnerships inside and outside your company should you reevaluate because they are not producing results toward your goal? What can you do about them?

10

Next Steps

"Hierarchies will come and go in shape-shifting forms resembling a swirl. Rock star leaders will be rare; networked leadership with strength and humility will work best. As centralized organizations become increasingly distributed, expect a cloudburst of disruption."

—Bob Johansen

You may know the Defense Advanced Research Projects Agency (DARPA) is a division of the U.S. Department of Defense that helps prepare America's defense with a focus on the future. To get more ideas and solutions for complex problems, they have held open competitions to see what innovations people outside the defense industry can develop. This is notable as even they, a group of very smart and creative thinkers, acknowledge they can't always come up with the best solutions for big and complex problems. An example of one of those competitions was in 2009 when they announced the Red Balloon Challenge. At the time they were looking to better understand communication networks to prevent a multiprong terrorist attack or a spreading disease.

The concept of this competition was to learn how fast people could organize, communicate, and find 10 red balloons placed around the U.S. This may not seem challenging, but the U.S. is 3,717,792 square miles, not including territories, and the balloons could be hidden anywhere. The balloons were a bit bigger than the usual birthday party balloon, but not by much. A $40,000 prize would go to the first group to locate all 10 balloons. Many people felt this was impossible. Remember Facebook had only launched four years prior to this competition and drones and personal flying devices were not in common use.

However, within a few days of the announcement, several teams had signed up to take the challenge. They represented hackers, social media entrepreneurs, tech companies, and research universities—groups of really smart and motivated people.

Just four days before the competition started, a late entry was made by a group from the MIT Media Lab. Coming into this competition so late, they realized they didn't have time to build tools, create a network, or really do anything that would resemble an organized approach to solving the challenge. Instead they built a website that had a simple invitation. It said something like, "When you sign up to join our team, you will receive a link with your name." The invitation asked you to have your friends sign up using your personalized invitation. This is where their model deviates from all the other teams. If someone who signed up through your invitation won, or if someone they invited won, you and everyone in the invitation chain would share in the winnings.

None of the other teams had this type of approach. The MIT Media group designed the rewards so they gave $2,000 per balloon to the first person to send the correct coordinates. Then the person who invited that person would receive $1,000, and $500 goes to the person who invited that person, and $250 to whoever invited them, and so on depending on how many invitations existed in the chain. You can see this is not a complex software application or sophisticated system, but rather a way of incentivizing people to connect with each other.

What happened? Two days before the challenge began, the MIT team switched on their website. At first nothing happened, but by mid-afternoon a few people joined, and then the connections began to expand rapidly. Membership exploded across the country even to Europe, which wasn't a part of the challenge. By December 5, when DARPA began the start of the competition, thousands of people had joined the MIT team.

The people at DARPA had estimated that it would take up to a week for a team to find all of the balloons. To everyone's dismay, eight hours, 52 minutes and 41 seconds later, all of the 10 balloons had been found! The MIT team won. There were 4,665 people who helped them.

Why did they win? One big difference was how they asked for participation. They said if you joined their team you would win money and your friends would too. The other teams who worked through their networks said something like, "If you join us you may win money." It was a competitive model, where if you found a balloon you would win and others wouldn't, so there was no incentive to tell anyone else what you knew.

The MIT model was very different because it encouraged greater participation, collaboration, and sharing information. The greater the participation, the greater the likelihood of spotting a balloon and winning. They wanted everyone in their model to benefit financially, even if they won a small amount.

It is a small difference, but it made a huge impact on how fast they could find the balloons. Their approach depended on people being honest, sharing, and cooperating with each other. For the participants, it was a fun game with a good possibility they could win money. This approach was not focused on individual success but on collaborative success.

Create an Effective Team

Consider what dynamics are created on a team when members compete with each other rather than cooperate. I am sure you have seen "lone rangers" or "rising stars" who work by themselves and don't share with others. Competition among team members destroys any trust as individuals work to "win" at the expense of others.

One way this happens is when a member of a team gives their leader information and doesn't give it to their teammates. It appears they are working to get the leader's favor. This would not be an example of a highly effective team. The leader, in these situations, can choose whether or not to share what they have learned with the rest of the team. In both cases, they lose the trust of the other members because it appears back channels or keeping information is the leader's strategy. On effective teams, trust is high.

Now transfer this behavior into a newly forming partnership or relationship with another company, such as in a merger or acquisition. What do you think happens to the trust between the employees from each company? This is generally considered a cultural problem, but to address it, we must examine what *kind* of cultural problem it is. What is causing the lack of trust? For example, we have covered authority, silos, behaviors, and leadership roles here.

Trust and honesty are values, not directives. Trust is not possible if people are not honest with each other. What happens if we feel others reject our idea or if we get angry for being ignored? We stay quiet and become a part of the "herd." Trust often takes time to build, and it is not a given when a team forms or a new person is hired. Trust is built with honesty. It you are the boss or team manager, and your team will only tell you things they think will please or not make you angry, they do not trust you. It's likely the best decisions are not being made. What happens when there is a crisis or pressure situation? To be a truly collaborative leader, you need a high level of trust among all participants.

When trust is a problem among hundreds of people rather than just a few, the inertia it creates is much harder to reverse. In its 2016 global CEO survey, PwC reported that 55 percent of CEOs think that a lack of trust is a threat to their organization's growth. The postmortems on many mergers often discuss culture clashes as a reason for failure—"culture clashes" is too broad a term, in my opinion.

Large factors we cannot control such as the economy, trade policy, or a natural disaster are hard to survive when you are alone. If you can develop trust and build durable relationships, those connections can help solve these challenges.

Building trust does require some vulnerability. It might come in the form of information sharing about internal workings, staff challenges, and lack of capabilities in particular areas. There will be bumps, disagreements, and collisions of ideas. However, by identifying and exposing vulnerabilities, more trust is built.

When solving problems, it's important to involve the people doing the work, as they know what is wrong and often have solutions. With mergers and acquisitions, the controlling company has all the leverage, and if they do not share it with those being merged, problems occur. Some companies view giving decision-making authority to the people doing the work as giving up control. This belief only results in chaos—you never have control over everything.

Engage in Your Ecosystem

Remember that in an ecosystem, there are multiple players that function with a dependence on each other, or else the ecosystem will collapse. This may look chaotic, as it is hard to see how one person affects another, but they have shared interest in working together. In the 2019 *Harvard Business Review* article, "In the Ecosystem Economy, What's Your Strategy?" Michael Jacobides developed five questions to be well prepared to operate in the business ecosystem. Jacobides' questions are summarized below:

1. *Can you help others create value?* An ecosystem relies on multiple players helping each other. If you do not contribute, you will not receive benefit in return.

2. *What role should you play in the ecosystem?* In the model for collaboration, remember it is not always best to be the star. More can be accomplished by working together and using each other's strengths, and leadership works best when it is shared.

3. *What should the terms for participation be?* Who has the authority to make decisions, and under what rules should the collaboration operate?

4. *Can your organization adapt?* Remaining flexible and resilient are important in the modern business ecosystem. While you must stay focused on your goal and purpose, you will likely have to make changes to your plan in response to circumstances that arise.

5. *How many ecosystems should you manage?* Keep your goal and purpose in mind whenever new opportunities arise. Ask yourself whether a new idea will benefit the purpose or if it is a distraction.

NEXT STEPS

Building an Ecosystem

It is easy to recognize an ecosystem that extends your business influence, and today it is easier than ever. Start the process the way Bamford, Baynham, and Ernst suggested: "A strategic examination of your current joint ventures and partnerships and the thoughtful creation of new ones can strengthen your position as you come out of the crisis and help you tap opportunities for growth during the coming rebound." (*Harvard Business Review*, 2020)

An example is building a supportive community that can act as a sort of sales team. In the article by Bussgang and Bacon titled "When Community Becomes Your Competitive Advantage," they examined a new business model that includes a larger ecosystem (*Harvard Business Review*, 2020). They provided two examples: SalesForce and Harley Davidson.

SalesForce did not build its $140 billion valuation through innovation of its software. They created a community that now has nearly 2 million members who support each other, organize events, produce content, and are a critical part of the global enterprise. The community is a network of talent providing support to SalesForce. The network is better than employees because they are using it in their own ways and are testing it, all the while helping others use it. SalesForce expanded their ecosystem to include its users as a community and benefitted greatly.

Harley Davidson has created and supported more than 1,400 local chapters around the world. The members of the chapters host events, discuss bikes, and connect online. They are a group of committed customers and they help promote the brand. This type of customer interaction is starting to become more common in businesses but is not widespread.

Smaller entrepreneurs often do this through social media to build their customer base before launching products. Then they engage those people to help sell the product. This strategy is better than hiring salespeople, but remember the motivation of these people is different, so think about why they are interacting with you.

How do these communities work? The management of these groups is primarily handled by the group members themselves and sometimes a designated leader. However, companies that have these community interactions do have people who act as an interface between the group and the company.

Bussgang and Bacon researched these groups and gave seven key elements of successful community groups. This list will look pretty familiar by now.

- A shared purpose

- Simple, easily accessible value consumption

- Simple, easily navigable value creation

- Clearly defined incentives and rewards

- Carefully crafted accountability

- Healthy, diverse participation driven by good leadership

- Open objectives, governance, and evolution

These community groups align with the collaboration model in that they have a goal, team members, actions, and attention.

Chaos in the Ecosystem

To be effective with this collaborative model, your organization will have to be more inclusive as you allow more people to interact with you. These people are not necessarily "controlled" in the traditional chain of command.

The business ecosystem is present whether a company wants to interact with it or not. The collaborative model allows you to design a way to interact better within the ecosystem. It may seem difficult to manage the model for collaboration and maintain control. Collaborative leadership distributes control and develops connected leadership because the system is just too complex to manage in a traditional sense.

A different style of leadership is needed, but that doesn't mean there isn't a flow of information up and down the organization. Accountability is not lacking. If team members fail to deliver, they fail too. That is incentive and accountability to me. Accountability has to be shared, and people won't be able to blame "the system" above them or below them because they *are* the system.

It is unlikely any company can control all aspects of a supply chain or the partners they work with. However, with multiple partners or alliances, there may be solutions that you never thought of and innovation can prosper.

When there is a challenge or a mistake in a collaborative project, handle it as "reparations," including forgiveness, follow-up actions that repair the situation, and preventative measures so it doesn't happen again. This type of non-punitive action can help a collaboration hold together in times of stress. Mistakes will be made. Rather than blaming others, accept the problem, repair it, investigate how to prevent it in the future, and move forward. One method broadly used for identifying the steps to take after a mistake is through an after action review or similar review process. The after action review is a review or debrief process for analyzing *what* happened, *why* it happened, and *how* it can be done better by the participants and those responsible for the project or event. It was developed by the U.S. Army, and there are informal and formal ways to use it. Because you never have complete control over what happens, authority is always shared. Similarly, accountability needs to be shared across the ecosystem, which allows corrections to be made without blame. You can and should learn from these reviews and improve performance.

In some nonprofit organizations, there are many volunteers who play a critical role in helping the organization complete its mission. I lead one organization with almost 1,000 volunteers from the board level to individuals who had direct involvement and sometimes decision-making authority. Decisions made by volunteers had the same weight as decisions made by employees. These volunteers can also walk away if they don't like what is happening. In this case, placing blame is not helpful. Establishing commitment is better.

A different take on this concept is Apple's standards for app developers. The decisions for which apps to develop are made in the developer's company, not at Apple. They get guidance, parameters, information, support, and opportunities for their voice to be heard. Apple has the last say about whether an app is accepted. What drives the developers is the success of Apple and how their success has a role in it. Purpose is the key driver of accountability.

Knowing where accountability lies is also helpful. If they know what they need to do, when it must be done, and what resources and information they need, then they can measure how successfully they met the task.

Volunteer committees and app developers are led from several levels. The committee or group has a leader, the group has an organizational contact, and finally there is an organizational leader. All these people must be aligned to the organizational purpose, have clarity in their work, and have support and accountability for their tasks.

Collaborative leadership is possible. I hope you feel excited about the possibilities. The rewards are enormous on many levels: commitment, revenue, engagement, and growth.

You may be familiar with the mantra that was used in England during World War II on a safety poster: "Keep calm and carry on." The poster was commissioned in 1939 by the temporary Ministry of Information in England. When things seem to be going off the rails, *keep calm and carry on*. Don't be afraid of what may seem like chaos. Focus on what you want to do, how to get it done, what support you need, and the benchmarks for accomplishing the tasks. Good luck, and have some fun collaborating with others.

Reflection

Personal Steps

If you want to boost your collaborative muscle, here are some things you can do to help others.

1. Begin to map your supply chain as far as you can, including all the participants. Then look for any opportunities for innovations or collaborations.

2. Find a nonprofit whose mission you believe in and join the board of directors. Listen and test the concepts. Is there organizational purpose? Is there clarity about the tasks? Is there support for the work? Is there accountability? A nonprofit board can be a good place to start because they generally move much slower than businesses, allowing you to first observe and test your ability to collaborate.

3. Look for a cross-departmental project or committee you can join. Observe and look for the purpose, clarity, support, and accountability. Assess how they are doing.

4. Look for someone outside your normal sphere whom you have wanted to work with or an organization where you know someone. Try out a small joint project. Outline the purpose, be clear, establish support, and have some sort of accountability.

Team Steps

If you want to explore and boost your collaborative muscle with a team or with your company, here are some steps you can take.

1. Explore the idea with your team. Discuss opportunities that you are currently missing because of human or financial capacity. Narrow your list to two or three that would have strong meaning and create drive within your company. (Not every-

one on your team may think of it this way, but that is okay.) This may take some time and you can also float the ideas by other people in your company. Also run the idea by people who you or the team thinks might be good to work on it and see how they feel.

2.   Reach out. Set up meetings with individuals, departments, or companies that have the capacities or expertise that you are lacking. Discuss the potential for a collaboration and push the idea more than you might normally in such a meeting until you come up with a potential goal that will resonate with both parties. Discuss the goal with others at your company. Then meet again to refine it. If it seems too hard to find a goal, then move on. There will be plenty of tense moments in a collaboration, and if you can't get started well, it will be even harder once you are in the middle of it.

At this stage, determine how much each organization, team, or person is able and wants to do in the collaboration. This helps you determine the decision-making process.

3.   Set up the team. If you have a goal that is agreeable, work with your team to identify and select the right people to work on it. You may be included or not. Assemble the team and discuss how they want to work together and ensure they are committed to the collaboration.

4.   Determine how to make decisions. Once you establish the decision-making process, it will make things go smoothly. The collaboration may be outside of the normal departmental structures and the leader may have different reporting structures. If another organization is involved, they should also do this or fold into your structure. Either way, they should have

some decisions they are responsible for. If the collaboration is a big effort, ensure the CEO knows about it and supports it. Find ways to push leadership to all levels of the work.

5. Make your plan and work the plan. Involve the key players in the more detailed planning. Identify milestones and understand when they should occur. Then begin working the plan. Be aware that new efforts, groups, or changes are likely as things move forward. You want to be able to adjust and evolve as the work necessitates.

6. Pay attention. If you built in milestones and benchmarks, this will make paying attention easier. Ensure you have metrics that make sense and are incentivizing rather than demotivating. Identify some places in the collaboration where work will be celebrated. Do not wait for an annual event. Smaller celebrations help keep people going. Do not forget to keep your eye open for new opportunities that will enhance the work.

Conclusion

"In ecosystems, stability and change are entangled with each other: Stability is achieved only through change and vice versa."

—David Hurst

So many things in our lives run in cycles: the school year, seasons, and the tax year. Natural ecosystems have cycles, too, and they also have many smaller cycles within the larger system that start and stop. Those cycles have to be maintained or the whole system will begin to fall apart. Plants grow, die, and decay, enriching the soil so more plants can grow. Some animals have to eat plants. As long as they grow and thrive, the animals can too. If one part of the larger system is removed, it could lead to a collapse. As in nature, the business ecosystem has some larger and many smaller cycles. If the smaller ones begin to fail, then the larger ecosystem can be affected, sometimes categorically.

Collaborations protect against the failure of ecosystem cycles. For example UPS, FedEx, or USPS could operate without manufacturing businesses but having a manufacturer as a customer creates a great benefit for them. If a transportation company goes out of business, the manufacturing businesses are in trouble until they can find other methods for delivery of their products. One system—transportation—can survive without one customer—the manufacturer—but that customer can't survive without the transportation. Pay attention to the relationships and who needs whom more in a collaboration. It highlights the need for a common goal between collaborating companies. Dependency is perilous if even one party is not paying attention.

Amazon has begun to develop a plan B—it is well known that they have begun their own delivery system. They have a few brick and mortar stores and many delivery trucks, and they are experimenting with drones and other unmanned vehicles. These alternatives allow them to be prepared for a breakdown in the current systems or to leapfrog over the existing systems to boost their capability. Either way, they are creating their own business ecosystem and cycles. Most businesses do not have the resources Amazon has. However, looking for partners can hedge against changes in the business ecosystem. Are there cycles or relationships you can look to for new opportunities?

In nature, opportunism is common. When a new species is introduced in an environment—often by humans—the new species often prospers unimpeded. If the newly introduced species survives, it will change the existing system. These are labeled invasive species or non-native species. What do we call products or processes in business that change the ecosystem? Disruptive.

Disruptive companies or efforts have a similar pattern to invasive species. They want to survive in the new system and can cause disruption to those that already thrive there. Disruption is common, and it should be expected. If a business is not preparing for disruption, they are at risk in the marketplace. Collaborating helps you remain flexible and resilient when the ecosystem is disrupted.

CONCLUSION

Research at Stanford by Walton found that working together also boosted the motivation of employees. A recent survey conducted by Dropbox.com found 87 percent of respondents said they needed to meet the varying collaborative working needs of different teams.

My hope with this book is to help leaders think differently about how they identify, assemble, implement, and pay attention to the systems of their businesses, internally and externally. I hope leaders will leverage the abilities and intelligence of others inside and outside their organization. Collaborating in this complex ecosystem allows a business to be more flexible, adjust, test, and launch new ideas and products.

Gathering others' ideas and opinions who can help you identify gaps and needs in your business is critical today. Complex problems are multi-dimensional and sometimes multi-disciplinary, making it difficult for one person and sometimes even one team to see the whole picture. Zooming out and zooming in.

Some companies have established innovation teams. Some are internal to the company and others are not. Another approach is to encourage everyone within a company or team to be an innovator. Whatever approach is chosen, it is beneficial to have some structures to allow ideas to circulate and be evaluated by others. Being systematic and occasionally unsystematic may create better results.

A good collaborative initiative begins with awareness of your strengths, capabilities, and weaknesses. Learn these aspects of yourself before you are in crisis. Know your value. Identify gaps and opportunities. Build a team for the problems you want to solve. Get the right people in the right places and zoom out to envision the growth you may experience by collaborating. When you do it well and leadership is shared, collaboration is powerful and can begin to take on a life of its own.

References

Baiya, Ph.D., Evans and Price, Ron. *The Innovator's Advantage: Revealing the Hidden Connection Between People and Process.* Aloha Publishing, 2017.

Bamford, James; Baynham, Gerard; and Ernst, David. "Joint Ventures and Partnership in a Downturn," *Harvard Business Review*, 2020. https://hbr.org/2020/09/ joint-ventures-and-partnerships-in-a-downturn

Barsade, S.G. "Emotional contagion in organizational life," *Research in Organizational Behavior*, 2018. https://www.sciencedirect.com/science/article/abs/pii/S0191308518300108

Benjamin, David and Komlos, David. *Cracking Complexity: The Breakthrough Formula for Solving Just About Anything Fast.* Nicolas Brealey Publishing, 2019.

Bradley, Amy and Olivier, Sharon, "How Engaged Is Your Team, Really?" *Harvard Business Review*, 2019. https://hbr.org/2019/10/ how-engaged-is-your-team-really

Brandenburger, Adam. "To Change the Way You Think, Change the Way You See," *Harvard Business Review*, 2016.

Brown, Brené. *Dare to Lead: Brave Work. Tough Conversations. Whole Hearts.* Random House, 2018.

Bussgang, Jeffrey and Bacon, Jono. "When Community Becomes Your Competitive Advantage," *Harvard Business Review*, 2020. https://hbr.org/2020/01/when-community-becomes-your-competitive-advantage

Chabris, Christopher, and Simons, Daniel. *The Invisible Gorilla: And Other Ways Our Intuition Deceives Us*. Random House, 2010.

Clayton, Byron C. "Shared vision and autonomous motivation vs. financial incentives driving success in corporate acquisitions," *Frontiers in Psychology*, 2015. https://www.frontiersin.org/articles/10.3389/fpsyg.2014.01466/full

Coffaro, David. "The Art of Inquiry," DaveCoffaro.com, 2019. https://www.davecoffaro.com/the-art-of-inquiry

Collins, Jim and Porras, Jerry. *Built to Last: Successful Habits of Visionary Companies*. HarperCollins, 2011.

Covey, Stephen R. *The 7 Habits of Highly Effective People: Powerful Lessons in Personal Change*. Simon & Schuster, Anniversary Edition, 2013.

Deming, Edwards W. *Out of the Crisis*, Massachusetts Institute of Technology, 1982.

Doshi, Neel and McGregor, Lindsay. *Primed to Perform: How to Build the Highest Performing Cultures Through the Science of Total Motivation*. Harper Business, 2015.

Duckworth, Angela. *Grit: The Power of Passion and Perseverance*. Scribner, 2016.

Dulhigg, Charles and Graham, James. "What Google Learned From Its Quest to Build the Perfect Team," NewTimes Company, 2016. https://www.nytimes.com/2016/02/28/magazine/what-google-learned-from-its-quest-to-build-the-perfect-team.html

REFERENCES

Epstein, David. *Range: Why Generalists Triumph in a Specialized World*. Riverhead Books, 2019.

Friedman, Zach. "Google Says the Best Teams Have These 5 Things," *Forbes*, 2019. https://www.forbes.com/sites/zackfriedman/2019/01/28/google-says-the-best-teams-have-these-5-things/

Gardner, Heidi K. and Matvaik, Ivan. "7 Strategies for Promoting Collaboration in a Crisis," *Harvard Business Review*, 2020. https://hbr.org/2020/07/7-strategies-for-promoting-collaboration-in-a-crisis

Gardner, John W. *Living, Leading, and the American Dream*. Jossey-Bass, 2003.

Goldberg, Amir; Corritore, Matthew; and Srivastava, Sameer B. "Duality in Diversity: How Intrapersonal and Interpersonal Cultural Heterogeneity Relate to Firm Performance," *Administrative Science Quarterly*, 2019. https://www.gsb.stanford.edu/faculty-research/publications/duality-diversity-how-intrapersonal-interpersonal-cultural

Grant, Adam. *WorkLife with Adam Grant*, TED, 2018. https://www.ted.com/podcasts/worklife

Greeven, Mark, and Yu, Howard. "In a Crisis, Ecosystem Businesses Have a Competitive Advantage," *Harvard Business Review*, 2020. https://hbr.org/2020/04/in-a-crisis-ecosystem-businesses-have-a-competitive-advantage

Hoffman, Reid. *Masters of Scale* podcast series (https://mastersofscale.com/). Barry Diller episode: https://mastersofscale.com/learn-to-unlearn/

"How to Improve Teamwork in the Workplace," *Gallup*, 2020. https://www.gallup.com/cliftonstrengths/en/278225/how-to-improve-teamwork.aspx

Jacobides, Michael G. "In the Ecosystem Economy, What's Your Strategy?" *Harvard Business Review*, 2019. https://hbr.org/2019/09/in-the-ecosystem-economy-whats-your-strategy

Jewell, Deb. "Today's Learner/Leader is Self-Directed and Intrinsically-Motivated," *Chief Learning Officer*, 2019.

Johansen, Bob. *Full Spectrum Thinking: How to Escape Boxes in a Post-Categorical World.* Berrett-Koehler Publishers, Inc, 2020.

Johansen, Bob. *The New Leadership Literacies: Thriving in a Future of Extreme Disruption and Distributed Everything.* Berrett-Koehler Publishers, Inc, 2017.

Johnson, Andy. *Pushing Back Entropy: Moving Teams From Conflict to Health.* Restoration Publishing, 2014.

Jones, Chris. *The DNA of Collaboration: Unlocking the Potential of 21st Century Teams.* Amberwood Media Group, 2012.

Johnson, Mark. "Digital Growth Depends More on Business Models than Technology," *Harvard Business Review*, 2019. https://hbr.org/2018/12/digital-growth-depends-more-on-business-models-than-technology

Konnikova, Maria. *Mastermind: How to Think Like Sherlock Holmes.* Penguin Group, 2013.

Levy, Moria. "Knowledge Retention: Minimizing Organizational Business Loss," *Journal of Knowledge Management*, 15(4), July 2011.

Markman, Art. "The Problem-Solving Process That Prevents Group Think," *Harvard Business Review*, 2015. https://hbr.org/2015/11/the-problem-solving-process-that-prevents-groupthink

Markova, Dawna and McArthur, Angie. *Collaborative Intelligence: Thinking with People Who Think Differently.* Random House, 2015.

REFERENCES

McGuinness, Jack. "Great Leadership Teams Optimize Collaboration," *Chief Executive Magazine,* 2019. https://www.relationship-impact.com/blog/ great-leadership-teams-optimize-collaboration

"Monthly Labor Review," U.S. Bureau of Labor Statistics, 2019. https://www.bls.gov/opub/mlr/2019/

Morris, Jill and Morris, Steve. *Leadership Simple: Leading People to Lead Themselves.* Improex International, 2003.

Parker, Clifton B. "Stanford research shows that working together boosts motivation," *Stanford Report,* 2014. https://news.stanford. edu/news/2014/september/motivation-walton-carr-091514.html

Pink, Daniel. *A Whole New Mind: Moving from the Information Age to the Conceptual Age.* Riverhead Books, 2005.

Price, Ron and Ennis, Stacy. *Growing Influence: A Story of How to Lead with Character, Expertise, and Impact.* Greenleaf Book Group Press, 2018.

"Redefining business in a changing world: CEO Survey," PwC, 2016. https://www.pwc.com/gx/en/ceo-survey/2016/landing-page/ pwc-19th-annual-global-ceo-survey.pdf

Renjen, Punit. "The Fourth Industrial Revolution: At the Intersection of Readiness and Responsibility," Deloitte Global and *Forbes,* 2020. https://www.forbes.com/sites/deloitte/2020/01/20/ the-fourth-industrial-revolution-at-the-intersection-of-readiness-and-responsibility/

Scott, Amy. "How Silos Damage Customer Experience," Matchboard, 2018. https://www.matchboard.com.au/ how-silos-damage-customer-experience/

Senge, Peter M. *The Fifth Discipline: The Art & Practice of the Learning Organization.* Random House, 2010.

Sheppard, Blair. "Six paradoxes of leadership: Addressing the crisis of leadership," PwC, 2018. https://www.pwc.com/gx/en/issues/succeeding-in-uncertainty/six-paradoxes-of-leadership.html?utm_campaign=sbpwc&utm_medium=site&utm_source=articletext

Sonnenfeld, Jeffrey. "With 'Stakeholder' Edict, Will Business Roundtable Catch Up With CEOs?" *Chief Executive*, 2019. https://chiefexecutive.net/stakeholder-edict-business-roundtable-ceos/

Surowiecki, James. *The Wisdom of Crowds*. Random House, 2005.

Thomke, Stefan H. *Experimentation Works: The Surprising Power of Business Experiments*. Harvard Business Review Press, 2020.

Voccola, Thomas. *The Accidental CEO: A Leader's Journey from Ego to Purpose*. Sea Fever Press, 2006.

Walton, G., Cohen, G., Cwir, D., and Spencer, S. "Mere Belonging: The Power of Social Connections," *Journal of Personality and Social Psychology*, 102(3), 2012.

Welch, Kyle and Yoon, Aaron. "Corporate Sustainability and Stock Returns: Evidence from Employee Satisfaction," *SSRN*, 2020. https://papers.ssrn.com/sol3/papers.cfm?abstract_id=3616486

Wilmer, Henry; Sherman, Lauren; and Chein, Jason. "Smartphones and Cognition: A Review of Research Exploring the Links between Mobile Technology Habits and Cognitive Functioning," *Fronters in Psychology*, 2017. https://www.ncbi.nlm.nih.gov/pmc/articles/PMC5403814/

Wiseman, Liz. *Multipliers: How the Best Leaders Make Everyone Smarter*. Harper Business, 2017.

Acknowledgments

This book represents a lifetime of lessons, whether positive or not so positive. Many people helped and counseled me over the years, some with a direct hand in influencing the content here and others with tips and strategies for leading or just "walking the walk." I have to start by thanking my wife, Diane, for putting up with me as a learner and divergent thinker—or in daily language, easily distractable. She listened to my stories, provided feedback, and accommodated my learning and leadership experiences. My two children, William and Charlotte, also have contributed by being supportive, listening, and voicing their ideas and experiences with leadership and offering specific suggestions for aspects of this book.

Special thanks go to two people who test-read parts of this book and offered suggested improvements: Ron Price and Jeremy Graves, Ph.D. Their insight and ongoing support during the writing process was invaluable and important.

And thanks to Whit Mitchell, longtime friend and now a colleague, who doggedly encouraged me to finish the book. The Price Associates team has been incredibly supportive too. My Mastermind group allowed me to try out ideas. I want to also thank the clients I work with and have worked with. They shared situations, examples, and strategies, allowing me to learn with them.

There are also a number of people who are not identified but their stories are in the book. I want to thank them as they were generous to speak with me about their perspectives and specific examples. They helped me see how approaches to leadership may be different but have similar principles and guideposts.

Many others along the way contributed to the development of my thoughts and actions as a leader through the years. These include a college president, a dean, and those leaders in our CEO Mastermind group in D.C. There are too many. I share good and bad examples of leadership in the book's stories to illustrate that the path of leadership is far from smooth and no matter how good we are, we have room to grow. I draw from others' work and research to validate and provide additional context.

And finally to the team at Aloha Publishing, who made this book happen even with my divergent mind, and believed in my vision for the book—thank you to Maryanna Young, Megan Terry, Jennifer Regner, and the design team. Without them, this book would still be just a notion floating around in my head.

About the Author

Francis Eberle has spent more than 25 years as an executive for nonprofit organizations and startups. He has successfully partnered with leaders and teams to create multi-organizational collaborations with long histories of accomplishments. His approach includes defining purpose, carefully choosing people with strengths and motivations to support the purpose, and listening and paying attention. He believes that people development is business development, and that the most effective leaders in the long run share their authority with others.

Eberle's approach to leadership grew from early leadership opportunities during his formative years, where he observed how others handled leadership authority and what successes or failures resulted from their efforts. He learned how to engage others to buy into team goals by crafting goals that achieved wins for everyone involved. He decided then that he would use his authority to support others, build capacity, encourage resolution, and solve problems. Those choices contributed to his successes in building a collaborative leadership style uniquely suited to helping teams adapt to constantly changing business ecosystems.

Eberle has entered every leadership position he's taken as if it were temporary. Reminding himself that every leader moves on helped him focus on the future of the organization rather than his own future.

He received a bachelor of science degree from Boston University, a master's degree from the University of Connecticut, and a Ph.D. from Lesley University. He has also taken leadership and nonprofit management courses from the Harvard Business School of Executive Management.

He is currently an executive coach and team dynamics specialist, helping leaders reflect on their own experiences and knowledge, and effectively connect to people and organizations to develop solutions to increase their performance. He works with a highly effective team of business and leadership coaches through Price Associates, where he is a leadership and organizational advisor.

He has co-authored three books in addition to writing *Connected Leadership: Engage Your Workforce to Lead Themselves*. He calls Phippsburg, Maine, home and writes in his home office at the end of a very long driveway, close to the ocean. He walks often with his wife, Diane, and their dog, Zoe.

Join the Collaboration

I am interested in your feedback on the topic of connected leadership and collaborating with leaders, organizations, and teams. Feel free to reach out to me at francis@price-associates.com and connect with me on LinkedIn.

Connected Leadership was the result of collaborations that began many years ago and will continue into the future, with the added contributions from readers, clients, and colleagues. At Price Associates, the community within TheCompleteLeader.org is a place where leaders can collaborate through educational resources and discussion points for executive coaching. *The Complete Leader* podcast expands these discussions and conversations.

As an author, I am always grateful for reviews on Amazon from others who appreciate this book. Reach out to me if you would like me to be a guest on your podcast or interviewed for your blog or media resource. Here are ways to connect and obtain more information and exercises:

- ▶ LinkedIn: Francis Eberle
- ▶ Website: Price-Associates.com
- ▶ Leadership resources: TheCompleteLeader.org
- ▶ For additional support materials:
  TheCompleteLeader.org/ConnectedLeadership

www.ingramcontent.com/pod-product-compliance
Lightning Source LLC
Chambersburg PA
CBHW030510210326
41597CB00013B/858